Diary of a Witness

Taking Christ to the Marketplace

By
Greg Daley

Acknowledgments

There are a few people I would like to thank for their support and encouragement in the writing of this book. First of all, I want to thank my beautiful wife and best friend, Mary. Your love, patience, faithfulness and sacrifice over these many years are a testimony of the grace of God in you. Who else would put up with me? You lived many of these stories with me, and having you as a partner in the grace of life is God's favor toward me. Thank you for always releasing me to fulfill God's call on my life. I love you so much!

To my son, Jerad, a true giver and servant of Christ who got the brains I always wanted. To my lovely daughter, Carrie, who has her mom's gift to administrate and a heart of compassion. I also want to acknowledge her husband, Jonathan, who is like a son and so much a part of our family. You guys are awesome! I could not have asked for a better son or daughter. What peace we have as parents when our children walk with the Lord. You made being a father seem easy.

Special thanks to Ann Bunker and Jessica Hammelman, for their encouragement and input in the first editing of this book.

To Joe McIntrye, thanks for your friendship and spiritual input into my life whenever I needed it. Thank you for your kind words about this book. Joe, you are a courageous man of faith whom I greatly admire. Also to Tim and Brenda Taylor, for your encouragement and for the love you show me and my family.

To my pastor, Gail Homan, thanks for believing in me and inviting me to join you and the team at SRC, where we are so blessed to experience the Father's love and presence. As a pastor, you are truly one of a kind. You believe in and bring out the best in everyone. As a friend of mine once said, "Who wouldn't want Gail as his pastor?"

Most of all, I want to thank Jesus, my Lord and Savior, Who redeemed my life from destruction, cleansed me with His blood, filled me with His Holy Spirit, and called me on a great adventure with Him to be a fisher of men. To God be all the glory!

Foreword

Times and seasons change, but the Word of God "to go into all the world and make disciples of all nations, baptizing them in the name of the Father and of the Son and of the Holy Spirit, and teaching them to obey everything I have commanded you" has not changed (Matthew 28:19 New International Version). Down through the ages, men and women of great faith have communicated this message through different methods and programs. Indeed we are all called to preach the gospel. It is an undisputable fact that God, in His love for mankind, has raised up men and women who have a call to communicate the message at the appropriate time. The mandate to preach this Good News is now more important than ever. It is not a lost art! I believe every human being is worth the effort. There is something very beautiful and dynamic that happens when ordinary people ask this extraordinary God to help them be a light to lost humanity. Something, which I do not fully understand, changes in the heavens, and we find ourselves thinking and speaking the heart of the Father to those made ready for salvation. This timely message to the church today is a real challenge to those who work in the marketplace. Opportunities abound every day, and we pass them by because we have struggled to witness, pushed the envelope, accomplished little and even offended people in the process. In some cases, we have exchanged a program of witnessing for the Holy Spirit-led conversion.

I applaud all the wonderful discipleship programs and witnessing tools the body of Christ uses. I am not against them. Many times people need a little book or manual to help them get started, but in the process, many times we have lost the art of listening to the Holy Spirit about men's souls. I believe as you read through this life of faith, you will find a man listening to the voice of God and speaking what he is hearing to those ready for salvation. God still uses our voice box. I know it has been overused in years gone by as we struggled to make our lives line up with what we were preaching. But today I invite you to dive in and allow yourself the delight of reading about the Holy Spirit challenging a man and following up with a manifestation of the gifts of the Holy Spirit. What a concept! Yet, the early church had this very concept, and thousands were saved by unlearned men speaking of the great works of Jesus of Nazareth.

It doesn't take a rocket scientist! It only takes someone bold enough to take God at his word and believe in his heart that God deeply cares for the lost. My prayer is that *Diary of a Witness* changes the way you think about communicating the Good News.

Gail Homan
Senior Pastor
Seattle Revival Center

Introduction

Years ago, a former pastor of mine said to me, "Daley, when are you going to write a book?" He made the comment after I had shared a few stories while speaking on the subject of soul winning. To be honest, writing a book to me seemed way out of my league of personal accomplishments, and besides, I thought, *Would anyone even care to read it?* But eventually, the Holy Spirit began to repeat the phrase, "You should write a book" through individuals I did not personally know. They just offered it as a thought to consider.

After too many encounters for it to be just coincidence, I decided to give it a try and sat down to recall the many different experiences I have had over the years of sharing my faith. I was surprised how easily the memories came back and the words seemed to flow onto the computer as I wrote of these things.

I wrote the book in a chronological order, sort of like a diary, beginning with how I came to Christ. That part is called **"My Story."** What follows is the section of the book titled **"His Stories."** I titled it that because I want to give Jesus the glory and honor due His name. These stories are not just about me, but me co-laboring with Christ in the harvest field. They are really His stories since without Him we can do nothing. I know that as I am an imperfect vessel, the outcome of every divine appointment or witnessing encounter is not always God's best; however, He is so able to take my weakness and shortcomings and make something good come out of it. His power is truly perfected in my weakness.

My prayer is that the Lord will take these simple stories and encourage and maybe even challenge you to step out and share your faith. Witnessing is fun. Sure, it can be intimidating at times, and I know there are others better equipped than I am, but the joy of seeing God touch a life is so rewarding that it drives out all fear of failure. May the Lord use this book to encourage you to proclaim the name of Jesus and see His kingdom come."

> And those who lead the many to righteousness
> will shine like the stars forever and ever.
>
> Daniel 12:3

Table of Contents

My Story   **1**

His Story   **5**

Story One: Empowered to Witness   5

Story Two: Driven From the Drive-in   7

Story Three: Won't You Be My Neighbor?   11

Story Four: Cementing Myself in Love   15

Story Five: Lady, What Did You Say?   21

Story Six: The Obscene Phone Call   25

Story Seven: Hit, Run and Pray   27

Story Eight: Out of Gas, but on His Way to Heaven   31

Story Nine: Happy Birthday! Love, Jesus   35

Story Ten: Parable of the Engagement Ring   39

Story Eleven: Highway to Heaven   43

Story Twelve: Selling Cars With Jesus   45

Story Thirteen: Adman for Jesus   51

Story Fourteen: Ragman for Jesus   59

Story Fifteen: Prince of Peace, Not Piece   63

Story Sixteen: Airline and Airport Stories   65

Story Seventeen: Mad Dog   79

Story Eighteen: Which Way to the Strip Clubs?   85

Story Nineteen: Hail Satan, No! Hail Jesus!   89

Story Twenty: Fresh Oil and Fresh Fire   93

Story Twenty-one: God and Godiva Chocolates   95

Story Twenty-two: "Frozen Chosen" or Chosen to Be
Frozen?   99

Story Twenty-three: Not the Magic Kingdom, the
Kingdom of God!   105

Story Twenty-four: "Pier" Pressure   107

Story Twenty-five: The Streets of San Francisco,
A Holy Ghost Production   113

Story Twenty-six: Fishing With the Net   125

Story Twenty-seven: Elmo's Fire   131

Story Twenty-eight: Painting Stories   137

My Story

*Therefore if anyone is in Christ, he is a new
creature; old things have passed away;
behold, all things have become new.*
                                    2 Corinthians 5:17

I was lying on the bottom bunk, watching helplessly as
two men brutally beat the young man just several feet away.
He lay on the floor with his nose broken and face covered
in blood. As they turned to walk out the door, they looked
over at me and said, "You're next!" I buried my head in my
hands and thought back to the events that brought me to this
place.

My father died while I was in grade school, leaving my
mom to raise five sons. Mom did the best she could, but I was
hurt and angry over the death of my dad. When I became a
teenager, I rebelled into a culture of drugs and crime. It was
the sixties, and every weekend, my buddies and I went to
San Francisco to hear the Doors, Jefferson Airplane, Jimi
Hendrix and others. In high school, a friend and I started
breaking into people's cars and homes. When we weren't
stealing, we were stoned or drunk. When I got out of high
school, I moved out and got my own place. It wasn't much,
but I had a nice car, a girlfriend, money in my pocket for
drugs to party with; this is what I lived for.

Eventually, because of my drug use, I couldn't hold a
job. I was out of work and out of money. My life seemed to
fall apart. I needed money, and I needed it fast. I devised a
plan to extort money from a local business in town. I thought
my plan was foolproof, but I was the fool. The FBI arrested
me as I was leaving the drop site where the money was to
be placed. They took me to jail and charged me with four
felony counts of extortion; I was facing five years to life.

In jail I began to think of what my life had become. I was a thief and a drug user. I only cared about me. I remember telling God if He would get me out that I would change. Because of a good lawyer and no previous record, I received three years' probation. I was free! Or so I thought.

Once out, I soon forgot about God. I was back with my old friends getting high. One night while driving home from a rock concert, I passed out at the wheel on the interstate. I woke up as the car careened off the road and crashed through a fence before coming to a stop. A couple came running over, yelling, "Are you okay? We've called the police, and they are on their way." I got out and was looking at the car. It was crushed up to the windshield. I was baffled because even though I wasn't wearing a seat belt, I was unhurt. Suddenly, I heard the words, "I spared your life." They were not audible words, but were very clear on the inside. God was trying to get my attention. When the police arrived, I told them my front tire blew and I lost control. Because the tires were bald and flat, they believed my story. God had spared my life, but I continued to reject His grace and to live for myself. It wasn't long before I violated my probation and ended up back in confinement at Santa Rita for a long stay.

I lay on my bunk bed, watching the young man who was just beaten struggle to get up. I did not know what to do. I tried to keep my mind occupied, so I picked up an old Readers Digest off the magazine pile and began to read a story about a woman who got trapped in her burning car after driving off the road and hitting a tree. She began praying to God for help. Out of nowhere came a man who pulled the door open and lifted her out to safety. He disappeared just as the firemen pulled up. Was this an angel? If God helped her, would He help me? I bowed my head and prayed, "God, please help me and get me out of this situation."

Suddenly, the door opened, and in walked four men who grabbed me out of my bunk and began to beat and kick me. I could hear cursing and feel the blows, but something strange was happening. I wasn't feeling any pain. Somehow I rose up and ran for the door. They grabbed my arm to pull me back but lost their grip. I went out the door and ran down the hall, yelling for the guards. Two guards came and took me to a room. They questioned me and then left. As I paced the room, waiting for them to return, I noticed a small mirror on the wall and went over to look at my face. To my surprise, there was not a mark on my face, and I was not hurt anywhere! It was then that I heard the Holy Spirit speak the words on the inside of me, "I protected you and got you out." God had answered my prayer! Sometime later, I was permitted to attend a chapel service, where I heard and understood the Gospel for the first time.

The preacher read from the Scriptures: "All have sinned and fallen short of the glory of God," and, "The wages of sin was death but the free gift of God is eternal life in Jesus Christ our Lord" (Romans 3:23). He went on to say that no man could be justified before God by keeping the law. The law was given so that every mouth may be closed and all the world may become accountable to God. Through the law came the knowledge of sin. I knew I was a sinner and needed forgiveness. He quoted 2 Corinthians 5:17: "Therefore, if any man be in Christ he is a new creature; the old things passed away; behold all things have become new."

He invited anyone who wanted to receive Christ to come forward. I went and prayed, inviting Jesus into my heart. I will never forget the feeling I had that moment as the weight of guilt and shame left and God's Spirit of love and grace came in. As I left the chapel and walked toward my barrack, I looked up into heaven as a new joy filled my soul. I began to cry with tears of gratitude for the joy I was experiencing. I remember thinking, *Lord, here I am in prison, and I feel so happy and free, yet there are so many outside who are not free because they don't know you.*

That was many years ago, and I can honestly tell you that Jesus Christ, Who changed my life then, is still so real to me today. He truly is the same yesterday, today, and forever. After being released from confinement, I eventually ended up in the Pacific Northwest, living and working in Seattle, and that's where I met Mary. Next to Jesus, meeting and marrying Mary has been the best thing that has ever happened to me. We started attending a Pentecostal church in west Seattle and were married. It was soon after that I had an encounter with the Holy Spirit that would change my life forever.

His Story

Story One: **Empowered to Witness**

*But you shall receive power when the Holy
Spirit has come upon you; and you shall be
My witnesses both in Jerusalem, and in all
Judea and Samaria, and even to the remotest
part of the earth.*

Acts 1:8

It was Sunday evening, and I had just walked out of the
sanctuary into the church foyer after the pastor had given the
altar call. He had been preaching on the baptism of the Holy
Spirit as something every believer needed in order to be an
effective witness for Jesus Christ. It was a good message,
but at that time, I just didn't know how to respond. Besides,
the part of his message about believers in the book of Acts
speaking in tongues seemed kind of strange. That was new
to me, and I wasn't sure about it. I hung around in the foyer
of the church and began looking at the gospel tracts in the
racks on the wall, studying each one and trying to decide
which one I might take and read later at home. I enjoyed
reading the tracts and seeing how each one would grab the
attention of the reader and then lead him to receive Jesus into
his heart.

I had a desire to tell others of Jesus and His power to
deliver from sin. However, I found the tracts more suited
than I was to share the Good News. Consequently, the gospel
tracts that I took home usually never left the house. As I
was going over the tracts, I heard an inner voice, one that I
would later recognize as the voice of the Holy Spirit, speak
these words to me, "Greg, I want to do something for you.
Go back inside." So I went back inside the service and knelt

by the front of the platform. The youth pastor came up to me and said, "You want to be filled with the Holy Spirit, don't you?" Not being sure what all that included but hungry for God, I replied, "Yes, I want all Jesus has for me." He went on to say, "I'm going to lay my hands upon you and pray, asking Jesus to fill you with the Holy Spirit. As He does, just begin to thank Him and speak forth in the language He gives you."

He spoke with a real confidence that something was going to happen, and all I needed to do was to yield. In my heart, I decided I was willing to trust God to give me all He wanted me to have. As soon as he laid his hand on my head, I felt what seemed like someone placing his hand on my jaw. I opened my eyes to see whose hand was on my jaw, and to my surprise, no one was there. There was a sensation of someone moving my jaw as if to prime a pump to give out water. I heard myself say several words that my mind did not comprehend. I understand having someone move your jaw may not be the usual way that people receive the baptism in the Holy Spirit. In Acts 2:4, they did speak with other tongues as the Spirit gave them the utterance, and there was a manifestation of fire upon them. I don't know if they felt what I felt.

I stood up from my kneeling position, and I could feel what seemed like electrical currents going through my body. My whole body seemed to tingle and come alive. Some of the people around me seemed to notice a change in my countenance and manner and remarked how the Lord had touched me. Although I had felt the presence of God's peace and love before, this was the first time I had experienced the power or the anointing of God in a very tangible sense. Someone even remarked to me that I "got it." I wasn't too sure what all I "got," but I knew something was different, and I would soon find out what, or more precisely, who that was.

Story Two: **Driven From the Drive-in**

And immediately the Spirit impelled Him to go out into the wilderness.
                                                        Mark 1:12

Then Jesus was led up by the Spirit into the wilderness to be tempted by the devil.
                                                        Matthew 4:1

In Mark's gospel, we read that the Spirit impelled Jesus to go, and in Matthew, He was led. I believe at times the Spirit will lead you, and at other times, you may be impelled, or driven. What happened to me after my experience in church that evening was more like I was being impelled or driven, rather than led.

After leaving the church service that night, my wife and I drove down the street to McDonald's to get a bite to eat before going home. While I was eating my cheeseburger, I looked out the window to see someone familiar to me go into a house across the street. The next thing I knew, I was telling my wife I would be right back, and then I arose, left the table where we were sitting, crossed the street and walked up to the door of the house. I knocked. When the door opened, a smell of smoke came toward me as the person at the door greeted me with caution. Someone in the background spoke up and said, "Hey, Greg, what are you doing here? Come on in and join the party!"

It was a voice from the past. An old friend I used to hang around with before I had committed my life to Christ was at this party. It was a time of drinking and drugs and late-night parties. I stepped in, and to my surprise, I boldly began to tell them about my experience of being filled with the Holy

7

Spirit and speaking in a language I had never spoken before. I then started telling them about Jesus. I hadn't been saved very long and didn't have a lot of Bible knowledge, but I just started talking. As I began to share, the people in the room stopped drinking and smoking pot. Soon several began to ask questions about what I had experienced. I began to share with them my personal testimony of coming to Christ and His love for them. Before I left, I asked if I could come back the next day and share more with them. They agreed, and the next day, I went back with my Bible and talked more with the couple who lived there about Jesus and the Holy Spirit.

This was my first encounter with the words Jesus spoke to His disciples in Acts 1:8: "But you shall receive power when the Holy Spirit has come upon you; and you shall be My witnesses." Never before had I experienced that kind of boldness and confidence.

The word "witnesses" in the Greek text is *martus* (mar'-toos). It means a witness, a judicial term. A witness in a court setting would then be testifying of what he or she saw and heard. In Acts 4:20, Peter and John said, "We cannot but speak the things which we have seen and heard."

This same Greek word *martus* is translated "martyr" in Acts 22:20. Stephen was stoned for his faith in Christ. A martyr then would be someone who dies for what he or she believes, someone who chooses to suffer death, rather than renounce religious principles. You and I are to *be* witnesses for Jesus Christ. Not just to witness, but to BE witnesses. In order to do this effectively, we need power. The disciples had seen and heard many things. After all, they had been with Jesus personally for at least three years, but He tells them to go to Jerusalem and to wait for the promise of the Father. Acts 1:8 says, "But you shall receive power when the Holy Spirit has come upon you; and you shall be My witnesses both in Jerusalem, and in all Judea and Samaria, and even to the remotest part of the earth."

The word "power" in the Greek is *dunamus* (doo'-namis). It's an ability, abundance, meaning might, a worker of miracles. Power and strength, a mighty, wonderful work. It usually implies a miracle itself. We get the word "dynamite" from this Greek word. Dynamite has the power to change physical circumstances once it is lit and explodes. God wants us filled with His power, and He wants that power to be unloosed so we can be effective witnesses of all Christ has spoken, done, and what He wants to accomplish through us. The apostle Paul tells us in Corinthians 2:4, "And my speech and my preaching was not with enticing words of man's wisdom, but in demonstration of the Spirit and of power" (*dunamus*).

We need the *dunamus* of God to speak God's Word with power and authority. We also need wisdom from the Holy Spirit to know when to speak and what to say. While it is true dynamite in the hands of a novice could be dangerous, I don't think we have to worry about God indiscriminately releasing His power at our will. I believe we work with Him, with the same desire the Son had when Jesus said, "Lo I come to do thy will." Mark 16:20 reads, "And they went out and preached everywhere, the Lord working with them and confirming the word through the accompanying signs, Amen." It is also true that our Father will train us up in the operation of the gifts as we desire and avail ourselves to Him. We are told in 1 Corinthians 14:1 to desire spiritual gifts, but I believe God still reserves the right to release their operation.

> But the one and the same Spirit, works all these things, distributing to each one individually as He wills.
> 1 Corinthians 12:11

As the Holy Spirit began to teach me to be a witness for Christ, I began to learn more about the gifts of the Spirit and how they were used to touch the lives of individuals and bring glory to God. There were many times when I thought it would have been a good time for a miracle, and yet God, in His wisdom, had something else in mind. He knows what is best for each situation. There is only really one way to grow as a witness for Christ, and that is by **being one**. No matter how inadequate or inexperienced we may feel, God wants us to begin to witness and to continue to trust and learn from Him. The Western mindset seems to be, Teach first and then do. The Hebrew thought is more in line with the kingdom of God, which is, Do first and then learn. It is said of Jesus in Acts 1:1, "of all that Jesus began both to do and teach." Many times I find people want to be taught and taught and taught before they ever step out and do. The Lord would have us many times simply step out in obedience and do, and, in turn, we are taught much. Even failure and mistakes can be a great teacher, if we stay humble and ask God to show us where we missed it and what we can learn from it. The Lord actually had me go back to the house whose door I knocked on and apologize to people for my arrogant approach because I challenged them on their beliefs with a lack of love and understanding. That was hard to do; the flesh fought me all the way, but it was worth it. It helped change me for the better. Being right is not always as important as doing the right thing.

Story Three: Won't You Be My Neighbor?

Then the Spirit said to Philip, "Go up and join this chariot."

Acts 8:29 NASB

And the Spirit said to Greg, "Go talk to your neighbor."

Greg's personal version

As I was in front of my house one evening, I noticed my neighbor, an elderly man, walking on the opposite side of the street toward me. Again, that still small voice spoke to me and said, **"Tell him about Jesus."** I hesitated for a moment, thinking, *I don't really know him, and what would I say, anyway?* Again the Spirit spoke, but this time stronger, **"Talk to him!"**

I crossed the street and greeted him, saying something to the effect of, **"Hi, my name is Greg, and I'm a born-again Christian"** (wondering what he would do with that). He looked at me with a nervous smile (probably wondering if I was safe) and then said he and his wife were of a certain denomination, but that their son was a devout Christian, and he was coming over to visit. He invited me into their home to meet his wife. Here I was, standing in my neighbor's house for the first time, and he is explaining to his wife my greeting outside. Both of them were religious but had never been born again. They told me about their son who was very involved in his church. When I asked them what church he went to, they mentioned a certain non-Christian church in town.

I was a new Christian and didn't know much about the other religions, but on the inside, I knew this older couple needed to know Jesus. I talked to them about how Jesus was

God Who became a man and died on the cross for our sins. I was amazed at how the Holy Spirit took what little I knew and began to give this older couple the words they needed to hear. I told them they needed to help their son know who Jesus was and that, as they read the Bible, they could check these things out. They thanked me for talking to them, and I left their home.

You know, looking back on that day, I really didn't know too many Scriptures, and I didn't know too much about his religious sect, but the important thing is I was learning obedience to the Holy Spirit's direction. God is so faithful to take whatever we have to offer, and if we trust Him, He can do mighty things. Many Christians feel they have to wait until they have all the right doctrine and right Scriptures memorized before they will ever step out and witness. One thing about beginning to witness after you get saved is that it will cause you to study God's Word so you can answer their questions. Many times it is not what we know but *whom* we know, and knowing Jesus is the most important thing.

When Jesus chose the twelve, it says in Mark 3:13, "And He went up on the mountain and called to Him those He Himself wanted. And they came to Him."

Do you understand you did not choose Him, but He chose you? And it says that "those He Himself wanted"! You are wanted by the Lord and for a purpose, and that is to receive the Father's love and to give it away. Verse 14 says, "Then He appointed twelve, that they might be with Him." The word "appointed" in Greek is a verb that literally means "to make someone into something by being with Him." That is what Jesus did with the twelve because the rest of the verse says, "and that they might be with Him and that He might send them out to preach, and to have power to heal sicknesses and to cast out demons." The authority of the disciples was based on a relationship with Christ. As we spend time with Him, we are changed and empowered to see His kingdom come and His will be done, for He said, "without Me you can do nothing" (John 15:5).

> Now as they observed the confidence of Peter and John, and understood that they were uneducated and untrained men, they were marveling, and began to recognize them as having been with Jesus.
>
> Acts 4:13

Did you notice it didn't say they recognized them as graduates of Jerusalem Bible College or Antioch School of Theology? I'm not saying that Bible school or any other type of formal training is not important or worthwhile, but what was important to note is that they had been with Jesus. That is the key. I believe the more time you spend with Jesus, the better equipped you will be to go and speak for Him.

We are telling others about a person. You cannot share about someone if you don't spend time with that person. Christianity is about relationship, not religion. I have a personal relationship with my wife, a marriage. It is not a religion. It is the same in our relationship with the Lord. We are the bride of Christ. We are to have an intimate and loving yet supernatural experience with a supernatural person, Jesus Christ. As a friend of mine has rightly stated, "The man with a biblical experience is never at the mercy of a man with a biblical doctrine." Doctrine is important, but duty to doctrine should not precede our love for God or for the lost. God has given to the church apostles, prophets, evangelists, pastors, and teachers, according to Ephesians 4:11, "to equip the saints for the work of the ministry," but waiting until you have a doctorate in divinity is not God's plan for being a witness. Having the head knowledge alone is not enough. If you want to be a witness, you need to be empowered by God and begin out of obedience with Who (Jesus) and what (the Word) you already know. This will cause you to pray and read God's Word and get to know Jesus, the Word made flesh, and to study the Scriptures for the answers to the questions people asked of you.

I believe God wanted me to plant seeds into my neighbors that He would then use to lead them to a saving knowledge of Jesus Christ. Sometimes we only get to plant seeds or maybe just water where someone else has planted. We must remember, however, that God will be faithful to give the increase.

Story Four: **Cementing Myself in Love**

Though I speak with the tongues of men and
of angels, and have not love, I am become as
sounding brass, or a tinkling cymbal.
                    1 Corinthians 13:1

Soon after I was filled with the Holy Spirit, the Lord
opened the door for me to go to work for a cement company.
Although it was very physically demanding work to begin
with, the pay was good, and it was close to home. My first
duty there was to stand at the bottom of a conveyer belt and
catch ninety-four-pound cement sacks as they came down the
conveyer slide and stack them on a wood pallet. It was sort
of a mindless job that kept me in shape. I was the new guy
working with a crew of five at this shipping terminal. I was
the only Christian there at the time. Two of the guys I worked
with, whom I will call Bill and Jay, made it their mission in
life to see if my belief and talk of Jesus was real by testing
me continually. The guy named Jay used to greet me each
day with a wave of his hand but did not use all his fingers.
Several hours a day, we would stack the cement sacks and
then take turns loading the bulk trucks whenever one came
through the gate and rang the bell. Loading a bulk truck was
a welcome break that usually took fifteen to twenty minutes
of time away from the stacking. This one guy catching sacks
with me started to take all the trucks that came in, leaving me
there to stack cement sacks alone. The other guy at the top
would drop the sacks faster than normal to make me work
harder when his friend was away. I would smile and just do
my best to keep up. As it got closer to the lunch break, I was
looking forward to the break from the lifting and the time to
read my pocket New Testament I took to work every day. I
was hungry for the Word, and I studied to effectively share

the gospel with those with whom I worked. As lunchtime approached, we all hoped that no trucks would come in to interrupt our lunch.

Just as it was time to break for lunch, a truck came in, and the guy who had been taking all the trucks, leaving me alone at the bottom of the catch table, turned to me and said, **"You can get it."** It was our lunch break, and he wasn't going to load any more trucks. I felt set up and used. *No way*, I thought. *You're not going to use me like that.* So I took off my hard hat and safety goggles and looked him in the eye and said in an intimidating voice, **"You go get the truck."** He looked at me startled and walked away. As soon as he walked away, my heart sank. Conviction! I felt like crawling under the catch table and never coming out. I had allowed them to get to me, and my flesh rose up to the point of me becoming angry with rage and willing to fight over it. I'm sure the devil was chuckling over my lack of fruit.

I finished sacking and walked into the restroom, looking for a place to be alone. I took the seat in the far stall and buried my head in my hands, saying, **"Lord, I really blew it."** I grabbed my pocket Bible I always carried and opened it to encourage myself. I stared in amazement as it fell open to these words:

> For the anger of man does not achieve the
> righteousness of God.
> James 1:20

How does God do that? I bowed my head and said, **"God, please forgive me for getting angry. I'm so sorry."** Immediately, peace came back into my heart, and then the Lord spoke to me to apologize to him. I really struggled with that. As a new Christian, I wondered what it would do to my testimony (as if I had one right now). I walked out of my seclusion into the lunchroom to see him sitting at the lunch table. I was glad we were alone. I looked at him and said,

"Bill, what I did out there was wrong. Please forgive me for getting angry at you like that." To my relief, he was very gracious. He probably felt his part wasn't right, either. He replied: **"It's okay. Nobody is perfect; we all make mistakes."** I said, **"You know, you're right, except Jesus was perfect and didn't make any mistakes, and my desire is to change and be like him."** And with that we changed the subject.

From then on our relationship changed for the better. The other worker, named Jay, never let up. He continued to give me that special wave of the hand. But God was changing my heart, and as I prayed for each of them, a real love began to rise up in me. Through the grace of God, it is possible to love our enemies and to pray for those who despitefully use us.

> But I say to you, love your enemies and pray for those who persecute you, so that you may be sons of your Father who is in heaven; for He causes His sun to rise on the evil and the good, and sends rain on the righteous and the unrighteous. For if you love those who love you, what reward do you have? Do not even the tax collectors do the same?" If you greet only your brothers, what more are you doing than others? Do not even the Gentiles do the same? Therefore you are to be perfect, as your heavenly Father is perfect.
>
> Matthew 5:44-48 NASB

As I prayed for Jay, the Lord would have me do things that would bless him. You know, in the world the philosophy is return evil for good, and even Christians at times will return evil for evil, but it is a holy thing when we return good for evil. As I prayed for the salvation of these men, the Holy Spirit would give me ideas to witness, not just in words, but in actions. I began to get the trucks that came in at lunchtime so they could eat uninterrupted. I would do whatever I could to make their job easier without complaining or trying to draw attention to myself. Jay, however, seemed to get worse and worse. He even would break things and blame it on me, but I was determined to just keep on praying and loving him.

One day I found out that his birthday was the next day. The Holy Spirit told me to bake him a chocolate cake for his birthday. So I told my wife about it, and together we made him this great-looking cake. I took it to work on his birthday, and you should have seen his mouth drop. He asked me why I did it, and I just smiled and said, "Because God loves you, Jay, and so do I." He didn't know exactly what to do with that, but eventually, his heart started to soften up. He would have his good days and bad days; he seemed so angry and depressed at times. I continued to pray for him.

I will never forget the day I was home and the phone rang, and when I picked it up, Jay was on the other end with the saddest voice, telling me his dog had been killed by a car. Here was this guy who never showed any emotion toward me other than anger or a fleeting grin, and now he was quietly weeping over the phone. He thought that God had killed his dog for all the things he did to me. I suppose I could have jumped on that one. However, the truth was, God loved him and cared for him and wanted to save him. I have seen many instances where those who are not seeking God seek out His people with whom they have a relationship and open up in times of personal crisis. Because of this crisis, I was able to pray with Jay over the phone for the first time, and the Holy Spirit softened his heart in a wonderful way. From then on, my relationship with Jay began to change.

Once in a while, my flesh would rise up and my attitude wouldn't always be right. But I found that if I would be honest and transparent, the grace was there, not just from God, but from the non-Christian workers toward me for being real. The Lord gave me great favor with my boss, and I worked hard never to bring reproach to the name of Jesus. Thank God for His grace and mercy; He knows our hearts, and even when we blow it, He is there to help us if we repent.

At one particular time, my boss was having a bad day, struggling with something, and he spoke to me with a sharp tone. I returned it with a harsh word instead of responding in love and understanding. I walked out of his office upset for the way he had spoken to me. As I was alone, I felt it again—the conviction of my heart to make things right—but I thought again of my credibility as a witness. Oh, how pride can deceive us! I told the Lord that my boss would never believe a word I said about being a Christian or knowing Jesus, but I couldn't get away from the thoughts that I had to make it right. I knew I had to talk to him, so I went into his office a few minutes later and told him I was wrong to speak that way to him and asked him if he would please forgive me for what I said. He turned to me, and with moisture in his eyes, said, **"Greg, now I know you truly are a Christian."** I was humbled by his statement and grateful I had repented. I realized again that Jesus called us to *be* His witness, not just to witness. Being a witness for Jesus is not trying to be super spiritual or have a "holier than thou" attitude, but allowing the Spirit of Christ to manifest and change our hearts and those around us.

The Passion Grows

One day I was driving to the store on an errand, and I reached over, turned on the radio, and tuned in to the local Christian station for some music. A song I had never heard before came through the speakers: **"I have a great, great joy in Jesus, and through me, Lord, it longs to be told."** As these words came through the speakers, the car was immediately filled with the glory of the Lord. The presence of the Lord was so strong I couldn't drive, and so I pulled over into a nearby parking lot and just started to weep and weep as the words of this song penetrated my heart. It felt like my heart was breaking for every soul who was lost without Christ. *What was happening to me?* I wondered, and eventually, His presence lifted and my emotions returned to normal. I believe God was changing my heart and imparting His love and passion for souls.

Story Five: **Lady, What Did You Say?**

*Walk in wisdom toward them that are without,
redeeming the time.*

Colossians 4:5

I was driving to the bank one day to get some cash. I pulled into the parking lot and got out of my car and headed toward the cash machine. I walked by a certain vehicle and heard a lady speak to me from the passenger side of a car. At first I wasn't sure my ears heard what I was hearing, so I stopped and said, **"Pardon me?"** She said the same phrase to me. It was then I realized she had propositioned me for sex. I said to her, **"Young lady, not only am I a married man, but I am a Christian as well, and I have given my life to Jesus."** She immediately became embarrassed and began to cry. She began to tell me she had known the Lord once but had long since been out of fellowship with the Lord and was doing this because she needed money to buy food for herself.

I told her God still loved her and that He wanted to heal her hurts and be the source for all her need if she would turn to God and begin to trust in Jesus from now on. She didn't think God could forgive her for the things she had done and was under much guilt and condemnation. I reminded her of the wonderful promise God gave us in the Bible.

If we confess our sins, He is faithful and just
to forgive us our sins and to cleanse us from
all unrighteousness.

1 John 1:9

When she heard these words, faith began to rise up in her heart, and so with confidence, she prayed as we came boldly to the throne of grace in prayer.

> Let us therefore draw near with confidence to the throne of grace, that we may receive mercy and may find grace to help in time of need.
>
> Hebrews 4:16

It was wonderful to watch the transformation of her countenance from pain to joy and peace. The Holy Spirit had begun a work of restoration. Afterward I told her my wife and I would love to help and bring her some groceries and see her get back on her feet. After getting her address and phone number, I left, thanking God for another opportunity to bring Good News to a hurting soul.

There are many people like this young lady who, because of one unconfessed sin or the other, have had their fellowship with God broken. Then the devil has kept them in condemnation, guilt, and shame, and from being restored to God.

Second Corinthians 5:18-20 tells us of the ministry we all have of reconciling the lost to the Father. Even if the person was once a Christian and is now not serving the Lord because of a besetting sin, he has lost his way. We can put him back on the path of abundant living. James 5:19 says, "Brethren, if anyone among you wanders from the truth, and someone turns him back, let him know that he who turns a sinner from the error of his way will save a soul from death and cover a multitude of sins."

> Now all these things are from God, who reconciled us to Himself through Christ, and gave us the ministry of reconciliation, namely, that God was in Christ reconciling the world

to Himself, not counting their trespasses against them, and He has committed to us the word of reconciliation. Therefore, we are ambassadors for Christ, as though God were entreating through us; we beg you on behalf of Christ, be reconciled to God.

2 Corinthians 5:18-20

In Colossians 1:20, Paul tells us of "the power of the blood to reconcile all things unto himself." To reconcile means to change mutually, to compound a difference, to bring two opposing things that are distant together to be one. Regardless of space or time. The blood of Jesus continues to do this nearly 2,000 years later! Did you know the Father has made provision for your future sins as well as the ones in the past. How do I know this? Because before you were born, Jesus shed His blood for you. It is never good to sin. It is better to do righteousness, but He has made provision through His blood to reconcile you, bring peace back into your heart, whenever you confess and turn from your sin. Colossians 1:20-22 says, "and through Him to reconcile all things to Himself, having made peace through the blood of His cross; through Him, I say, whether things on earth or things in heaven."

The experience with the woman at the bank reminded me of a word the Lord gave me as I worked with unbelievers, and how important it is that we take heed of our walk with Christ. In doing so, we save not only ourselves, but those who hear us. If we do not know who we are in Christ, and our hearts condemn us, if we are not in regular communion with the Holy Spirit, but are allowing the cares of this life or some fleshly sin to continue to beset us, how will we be secure in our own salvation enough to share it with others?

Pay close attention to yourself and to your teaching; persevere in these things; for as you do this you will ensure salvation both for yourself and for those who hear you.

1 Timothy 4:16 NASB

Story Six: The Obscene Phone Call

And these signs will accompany those who have believed: in My name they will cast out demons.

Mark 16:17

My family and I were just sitting down to eat dinner when the phone rang. "Hello?" I answered. The voice on the other end was that of a young male, and he began swearing and making obscene comments. "Wait a minute, don't hang up," I said. **"God loves you, and Jesus can set you free. Don't hang up! I'm a Christian, and the Lord can set you free from this spirit of lust. He wants to help you—will you let Him?"** There was a moment of silence on the other end. I must have startled him. I took the phone to the other room and continued to talk. "Jesus loves you," I said. "It's okay, don't be embarrassed."

The young man on the other end began to open up. "I don't know why I do this; I can't stop. Can you help me?"

"Yes," I replied. **"Jesus can set you free; let me pray for you right now."** I prayed, **"Father, I thank you for this young man, and in Jesus' name, I know You put us together so he could hear of Your love. Satan, I bind you in Jesus' name, and I command the spirit of lust and perversion to come out of this man and let him go!"** There was a sigh on the other end as the Spirit of the Lord brought liberty and freedom into his life.

"What's your name?" I asked. With a newfound freedom and peace, he began to tell me all about himself and even where he lived! I began to tell him the Good News, and then I asked him if he wanted to receive Jesus Christ into his life. He exclaimed, "Yes!" Soon after praying, we were both rejoicing. "Your name is now written down in the Lamb's

Book of Life," I told him. I encouraged him in the Lord and, after hanging up the phone, began to praise the Lord for what He had done.

When I returned to the dinner table, my wife asked, "Who was that, honey?"

"Oh, just an obscene phone call, but he repented and accepted the Lord." To God be the glory!

Lord, help us to remember always the power that is in the name of Jesus and to make the most of every opportunity to speak the truth in love and see the devil defeated again and another soul saved by the saving grace of Jesus Christ. Lord, help us to remember you are with us in every moment of our lives and to remember the fields are white for harvest.

Story Seven: **Hit, Run and Pray**

The earth is the LORD's and all its fullness,
the world and those who dwell therein.
> *Psalm 24:1*

The earth is the Lord's, the fullness thereof,
and the van that you are in.
> *Greg's personal version*
> *of Psalm 24:1*

It was a beautiful day as I drove through town in my brand new Volkswagen camper. I had just recently traded my Harley-Davidson in toward a new Vanagon. It was a little more practical for my wife and me than the motorcycle we presently used to get around, especially in Seattle. It was also great for the occasional weekend camping. I was traveling on a road that had two lanes in each direction. I was driving in the outside lane, following the road as it turned to the left.

Suddenly, the driver of the car on the inside lane next to me decided to make a right turn into a nearby bank driveway from the left lane. The car smashed into the left rear panel of the van and continued on into the bank parking lot. I pulled over and got out of the van, looking at the damage to the rear end. Three elderly ladies came over to me; one took off walking, and the other two began yelling, exclaiming how I had cut them off. "What do you mean?" I replied. "You can't make a right turn from a left inside lane!" Then I smelled the alcohol coming off her breath as she continued to blame me for her driving. I couldn't believe it. These two sweet-looking grannies smelling of alcohol were accusing me of causing the accident! I sighed and said, "Well, look, let's just exchange information and talk about it."

All of a sudden, the one who was driving said, **"My husband is dying in the hospital, and I have to get to him."** She turned with one of the other ladies and walked fast to her car and drove off, leaving the third one who had walked away on her own. Before I knew what had happened, they were both gone, leaving me there with a dent in my new van.

"Lord" I cried, **"What is going on! What do I do?"**

The Holy Spirit said, **"I want you to witness to that woman who was left behind."**

"How do I do that? I don't even know where she went."

The Holy Spirit replied, **"I'll show you."** I got in the van and looked around, but there was no sign of her. So I just drove down a street, came to a stop sign, and drove on to the next intersection and turned left. I drove down half a block, and there, to my surprise, was the lady, standing by a bus stop. I pulled over, rolled down the passenger window, and she exclaimed, "It wasn't my fault!"

I said, "It's all right. Can I give you a lift home?" She looked around nervously, then came closer to the door of the van and got in, and we started to drive as she gave me directions.

I prayed for wisdom and said, **"Look, I don't care about the van, but I am concerned about you and your friends."** (Imagine having to tell a woman who could be your grandmother to be careful whom she hangs out with.) **"You need to know that God loves you and wants to be a part of your life."**

She looked at me and with anger and in a bitter tone said, **"God doesn't love me. If God loved me, why did He take away my husband?"** The anger and hurt on the inside of her rose up. Apparently, she had lost her husband and was blaming God for it.

"Ma'am," I said, **"God understands your grief, and He loves you. He can take the place of the loss and fill your**

heart with love and peace if you will let Him."

She grabbed the door handle and yelled, "Pull over," so I pulled over, and she jumped out of the van.

I never saw anyone, especially at that age, move so fast. She quickly walked up the sidewalk and disappeared around the corner. I slowly drove up the street, thinking, *This is really weird*, when all of a sudden, the Holy Spirit came on me, and I had to pull over because of the tremendous burden that was coming up within my spirit. I began to weep and weep. I don't usually cry like that, but this weeping and groaning came up out of my spirit as the Holy Spirit began to make intercession for this lost soul through my cries and groanings.

> And in the same way the Spirit also helps our weakness; for we do not know how to pray as we should, but the Spirit Himself intercedes for us with groanings too deep for words.
> Romans 8:26

After the burden to pray lifted, I drove on home, thinking about the day's events. God longs to reach out and heal the hearts of those who are hurting, and oh, how He wants to set them free from their pain if they will only listen. When I got home, I looked at my new van and the dent in the back corner with a sigh. *I can't believe my van is crunched*, I thought to myself. "Whose van?" the Holy Spirit replied. I listened as God began to remind me I had dedicated everything I had to Him, even my vehicle. "Oh," I said as I remembered.

Sometimes we are so quick to make our vows or pledges to God concerning things we own, saying, "It all belongs to Him." Then we forget about it, and when a neighbor or a friend wants to borrow it, or, as the Scriptures put it, the Lord has need of it, we forget and take it back. So I said, **"Yes, Lord, all that I have belongs to you, and I trust you."**

Well, several weeks later, my wife was at a grocery store

when someone backed into our parked van and crunched the other side. The man was very apologetic and very responsible, saying he had auto insurance and would take care of it. When we took it in for repair, the auto body shop agreed to fix the other dent damaged by the lady at no extra cost. Praise the Lord!

Story Eight: **Out of Gas, but on His Way to Heaven**

Let your light so shine before men, that they may see your good works, and glorify your Father which is in heaven.

Matthew 5:16

My family and I were driving down the street headed home when we came across a bright red Chevy Camero with its emergency lights flashing. This was not your stock Camero! It had been converted into a street rod. It had a custom hood with quite a bit of the engine sticking out of the hood, all chrome. The owner put huge tires, chrome rims, and a very shiny red paint job into the car. He was also out of gas. It looked like a gas guzzler. I pulled my car up behind him and got out of the driver's seat. **"Do you need any help?"** I asked. He replied, **"Can you help me push it over to the curb?"** We pushed his car through the intersection and over to the right side, as my wife pulled our car over and parked behind us.

He didn't have a gas can, but he lived just down the street, and he could get one at his house and then get gas. I offered to take him, but he wouldn't leave his car alone for fear of thieves or vandals. He was very protective of it, and for good reason. I thought for a moment and then felt it was safe for my wife and kids to run him home while I watched his car. He was grateful and relieved, so he got into my car with my family, and they headed to his house. When he got back, he thanked me and asked me why we went to all that trouble for him. I told him we were Christians, and Jesus said to love one another.

He then began to tell me of a disturbing movie he had seen on television that made him fearful of life and his future. I

31

began to share about the security we have in knowing Christ and ministered the gospel to him. I asked him if he wanted to accept Christ, and He said, "Yes." We prayed, and the Lord came into his life.

It has been said that sometimes people don't care what you know until they know you care. When people see agape demonstrated, they usually want to know why. We can tell them it's because the love of God compels us.

Opportunity Is Knocking

I have found it to be true that if we start making the most of the opportunities that come to us to witness, the Lord will start arranging what I like to call "divine appointments." Whenever a salesperson comes to my house, I try to find a way to mention the Lord. Usually, this means you have to take the time to listen, which isn't hard since salespeople want to do all the talking anyway. After they give you their "sales pitch," you can get into a normal dialog and ask questions that can lead into the gospel. They usually will mention something that will spark a transition from the natural into a spiritual truth from God's Word. One door-to-door salesman who came to my door remarked how he was standing on the corner of my street and just about to go the opposite direction when "something," as he put it, compelled him to come to our house.

At other times, it's just fun to be bold and see what will happen. I was standing on the street waiting for someone when a man walking a little dog came up the sidewalk. I smiled and greeted him and then said, **"That's a cute little dog you have. Do you think there will be any dogs or animals in heaven?"**

He replied something along the lines of, **"Well, I don't know. I never thought about it."**

I followed up with, **"Do you know if you will be there**

to find out?" He replied he wasn't sure, which led into a discussion of the gospel. I've used that transition line in many ways.

To someone who is really into cars: **"Hey that's a nice car you have. Do you think there will be any cars in heaven? Do you know if you will be there to find out?"**

It's also a good line to use in elevators just to get people to think.

These are just some ideas that God will give us as we make witnessing or soul winning a priority. I have led people to the Lord using transitional dialogs and some into the fullness of the Holy Spirit baptism. Once in a mall, I was sitting, having a cup of coffee. Two young people came by and sat at the table next to mine. I noticed he had a particular baseball cap and remarked about the team. We exchanged a little small talk, and then he asked me where I was from and what I was doing in the area. That led to me pulling my chair closer, and we engaged in a little conversation. Pretty soon I mentioned the "C" word (church), and they kind of lit up. As it turned out, they were new Christians and just married. I began to talk to him about the Holy Spirit, and you should have seen her eyes light up. Without her saying anything, you could tell she was glad to hear another man talking to her husband about what she has been trying to share with him. Pretty soon we were praying, and he was asking Jesus to baptize him in the Holy Spirit. It was a great experience for all of us.

If we are looking for the harvest or opportunities to witness, God will send them. Actually, He will send them many times, even when we are not looking, but the problem is we tend to miss it.

> Do you not say, "There are yet four months, and then comes the harvest"? Behold, I say to you, lift up your eyes, and look on the fields, that they are white for harvest.
> John 4:35

That means people are now ready to receive the gospel if we will but lift up our eyes and look. Don't just be caught up in the cares of this life, but look for those that are white for harvest.

Story Nine: **Happy Birthday! Love, Jesus**

Driving home from the grocery store one evening, I noticed a young man on the corner selling flowers out in the rain. I thought about how difficult it must be to stand on the corner in the rain and wave flowers in your hand to try to earn a living. As I passed him by, the Holy Spirit spoke to me about that new umbrella I had just purchased. He asked me to take it to him and that there would be an opportunity to witness.

As I came in the house with the groceries, I asked my wife where the umbrella we had just bought was. She said it was in the closet and asked why I needed it. I told her what the Lord had said and remarked I would be right back. I asked her to pray for this young man as I headed out the door. When I returned to the spot where the young man was, I noticed that a van with a trailer had pulled up next to him, and someone was helping him put his flowers and gear away. I pulled over across the street and into the parking lot of a 7-Eleven convenience store, parking next to the phone booth. I sat there, with the car running and the windshield wipers going, watching as they loaded up his flowers and stand. I asked the Lord what I should do, thinking I was too late to do anything. It seemed as if the Holy Spirit was having me wait.

I was thinking that if I wait, I could miss an opportunity to witness as intended. As I sat watching, I continued to pray in the Spirit. Pretty soon everything was loaded up, and they got into the van to drive away. I really felt I had missed the Lord's direction on this one, and then, to my surprise, the driver got out and raised the hood and began looking underneath it. The van would not start. That's when I heard the Holy Spirit say, **"Now go over."** I drove across the street and got out, asking if there was anything I could do to help. He asked if I would take him down the road to where the rest of their workers were so he could get help. I told him I would be glad to. As I got back into my car, the Holy Spirit reminded me about the umbrella, and I grabbed it and went over to the van.

There were several other young men sitting in the van. I handed it to the one who was working that corner and said, **"Here, Jesus told me to give this to you."** He looked at me very surprised and with a big smile said, **"You know, today is my birthday, and this is the only present I have received today. I really wanted one of these but was unable to buy one right now."** I told him God knew it was his birthday, and the Lord knew what he needed. That gift really touched his heart and let him know how much God cared for him. After giving him the umbrella, I got into my car with the one who was the foreman, or person in charge.

We started driving down the road, and he again thanked me for coming to their aid. I said I was happy to do so and asked Him if He would like to hear some Good News! He replied, **"I could use some good news."** I told him the Good News was that God was in the person of Jesus Christ, not counting our sins against us, but nailing them to the cross where Jesus bled and died in our place.

I told him that God sent his Son Jesus to die for our sins and that He also rose from the dead to give us eternal life if we will believe in Him. I shared the rest of the gospel with him, and He replied, **"That is good news."** I asked him if he would like to invite Jesus Christ into his life, and he said, "Yes." He prayed with me, asking God to forgive him for his sins, and then I led him in a prayer receiving God's forgiveness and confessing Jesus Christ as Lord and Savior. We rejoiced together in the grace of God.

It seems so easy, yet every time it is a miracle. Who knows how many times this person had been witnessed to, or what his background was, or who was praying for him. If we will partner with the Holy Spirit, He will direct us to those whose hearts are prepared. Acts 5:32 says, "And we are His witnesses to these things, and so also is the Holy Spirit whom God has given to those who obey Him."

Notice that we are not alone. The Holy Spirit is with us, and so we are not witnessing all alone. Notice, however, He is given to those who obey Him. It's important we are willing participants and submitted to His leading. I remember pulling into a gas station one day, and as I got out of the car, the service station attendant looked at me and said, **"Hey, what's the good news?"** What would you say? I know what the Holy Spirit had me say.

Story Ten: **Parable of the Engagement Ring**

*Then He spoke many things to them in
parables, saying, "Behold a sower went out
to sow."*
                          Matthew 13:3

*Using the boat as a pulpit, he addressed his
congregation, telling stories. "What do you
make of this? A farmer planted seed."*
                          Matthew 13:3
                          The Message

Many times as Christians, we tend to use words or
phrases to communicate the gospel that are churchy or what
we might call Christianese. They are biblical and good, such
as "redemption" and "sanctification" and "born again," but
sometimes they do not communicate to the non-believer in
a way that they can relate. Jesus used stories that got the
attention of the people and explained kingdom truths in a way
they could grasp and understand. On one particular occasion,
the Holy Spirit began to teach me how to incorporate a story
that would relate to the listener and bring a truth that would
hit home. I called this story "The Parable of the Engagement
Ring."

One afternoon I walked into a gym at my neighborhood
recreation center to work out. Since it was free, and usually
not used by many people, I would visit it often and put in
a thirty-minute workout. When I walked in, this lady was
pedaling on a bike machine. She greeted me with a smile
and said hello. I said hello back and went into my usual
workout routine. She seemed to want conversation and made
comments about the weather and local sporting events. I,

quite frankly, was in a hurry to just get my routine done and leave.

She was very energetic and talkative. She talked about her job and her husband, and about travel and health and on and on. I nodded or grunted during reps. (I was just wanting a quiet workout.) When I was done, I said goodbye and left thinking about her. She seemed truly happy and fulfilled, she seemed so alive, yet in my heart I wondered if she had a personal relationship with Jesus. This Bible verse in Proverbs came to mind: "There is a way which seems right to a man, but its end is the way of death" (Proverbs 14:12).

I decided to pray for her and trust the Holy Spirit to give me the right words she needed to hear. When I returned two days later, I found the little gym empty and began my workout. Not too long into my routine, this bouncy, petite lady came walking in again. She immediately struck up conversation as if we had been neighbors for years and were just catching up on the news of the day. The more she talked, the more I learned she was really into health and right living. She seemed to be a very positive person.

Jesus said out of the abundance of the heart the mouth speaks. All you have to do is just listen to someone long enough, and you will know what he believes. And believe me, this lady could talk!

Finally, the Holy Spirit began to nudge me about witnessing to her. Lord, what should I say? **The Spirit reminded me of a story I heard and prompted me to tell it to her. So I began to tell her this story:** "There was a certain man who fell in love with a beautiful woman and one day after a time of courtship decided to propose to her and ask for her hand in marriage. He took her out to a romantic place for dinner and wined and dined her, and when they were both finished eating and relaxed after their wonderful meal, he took out a little tiny box and handed it to her with great anticipation for her reaction and reply. She took one look at the box, and her eyes got real big and glassy, and then she slowly opened it to behold this beautiful, big, shining diamond set in a gold ring. She lifted it out of the box, and to the shock of the young man, she tossed the ring aside and held up the box and declared, "What a beautiful box! This is so wonderful!"

Then I looked this lady in the eyes and said, "You know, as crazy as that sounds, there are people today who are so concerned and pay so much attention to this body of ours, this box, so to speak, pampering it and idolizing it, that they forget that it's what is on the inside that holds the true value. This body of ours is only a box, and one day it will die and rot in the ground, but what about the soul that goes on to live forever? What does it profit a man to gain the whole world and lose his own soul, or what can a man give in exchange for this soul? **You see, physical exercise is good, but spiritual exercise profits you more, for it holds in it the ability to bring life to the soul.**"

Well, I had her attention, and she was visibly shaken by this parable, and so sensing the leading of the Holy Spirit, I began to ask her about her spiritual background. **"Tell me,"** I said, **"if you were to die tonight and stand before God and He was to say to you, 'Why should I let you into My heaven to live with Me forever?' what would you say?"** Well, as most people do, she told me of her good intentions and how she had always tried to do what was right. After all, she never killed anyone. So I began to share with her that the Bible says that all have sinned, and the wages of sin are death. That, according to the Bible, we are saved by grace through faith, that not of ourselves, it is the gift of God, not of works, lest any man should boast (Ephesians 2:8-9). I explained that if we could work our way to heaven, then Jesus died in vain. Only his death and sacrifice alone could make us righteous before God. If we would simply agree with what God has said in His Word about our spiritual condition and believe what the Bible says Jesus did for us in that He bore our sins and shed His blood for our redemption, we could know that our sins are forgiven, and by repenting of our sins and asking Him to forgive us and come into our lives, we would receive eternal life. For eternal life is in a person; His name is Jesus.

> These things I have written to you who believe
> in the name of the Son of God, in order that
> you may know that you have eternal life.
> 1 John 5:13

So I asked her if there was any reason why she couldn't ask Jesus into her life and begin trusting Him, now as Savior and Lord. She nodded her head and said, **"Yes, I would like to know."** So, sitting there on the Universal Weight Machine, she had her burden of sin lifted as she asked and received God's forgiveness for her sins and gave her heart and life to Jesus.

The Holy Spirit is so faithful to convict the world of sin and of the availability of righteousness through the triumphant work of Christ and the defeat of Satan to prove the certainty of judgment (John 16:8). So now she not only had a body that was physically fit, but, more importantly, a soul that was fit for heaven!

Lord, help me believe the Word that You spoke, that if I would follow You, You would make me a fisher of men. And help me to be obedient. Amen.

Story Eleven: **Highway to Heaven**

Driving down the road one day on my way to a lumber store to pick up some items for the home, I heard the Holy Spirit say, **"You are going to see a hitchhiker after you make the right turn. I want you to give him a ride and witness to him."** When I turned right at the next intersection, there he was, half a block up the road with his thumb out. Now let me say, I don't believe it's always wise to pick up strangers, but when the Holy Spirit tells you you're going to pick up someone before you see him, you're pretty safe. So I pulled over, and this guy, in his late twenties, who was trying to get to work, got in. He was fairly talkative, and he spoke of the usual things people do, such as the weather and so forth.

I went for the direct approach and told him I was a Christian, and the Lord had spoken to me to pick him up before I had seen him. He found that to be very interesting. I also told him I would take him to where he was going if he liked. From that moment on, I began to share the Good News with him about God's love for him and how he needed to give his life to Christ. I was planting seeds into his heart as the Holy Spirit led. Finally, we reached his destination, and I asked him if he wanted to give his life to Jesus. He said, **"Not at this time,"** but he would think on the things I had spoken to him about. He got out of the car and thanked me for the ride. I began to pray for him as I drove away, asking God to water the seed that was planted and to bring him into a saving knowledge of faith in Christ. Sometimes that is all we can do. If we are faithful, it is all we need to do; God will do the rest.

Another time I was driving in my car and was about to enter a freeway on-ramp when I saw two young girls with backpacks and a sign reading "Heading East." I was heading east several miles to another exit to go home. Again I felt the Holy Spirit impress me to pick them up. I pulled over, and they got in the car with all their stuff. I said, **"You girls look like you are going camping,"** and they said, **"We are! We're traveling across America."** I felt immediate concern for their safety and began to pray, asking the Holy Spirit to help me speak what they needed to hear. I spoke to them briefly of the dangers of traveling in the time we are living in, but that if they had a mind to do it, they needed to go with the presence and blessing of the Lord, and He would protect them.

To my surprise, they were both very interested in knowing about the Lord, so I told them about Jesus and all that He did for us at Calvary. This took some time to talk in detail, so I told them I would take them to the highway heading east and leave them by a good on-ramp. By the time we got there, the Holy Spirit had done His work, and they were both ready to receive Christ into their hearts. We pulled over, and they both prayed the sinner's prayer, asking Jesus into their lives. I then prayed a prayer of protection, asking God to place his angels around them all the way. I gave them each a tract to read, and they left the car, thanking me for the ride and the Good News. I left, thanking God these two girls were not alone anymore and that He was with them.

Story Twelve: **Selling Cars With Jesus**

Eventually, the Lord began to speak to me about leaving the cement plant and going into sales. I believe it was to be further training for what He was calling me to do. When God begins to speak to you about a change in direction or a job change, you usually begin to hear Him say it several times, or it is confirmed from several sources. "In the mouth of two or three witnesses let every word be established" (Matthew 18:16). It would happen that I would be somewhere and overhear a couple of car salesmen talking, and my spirit would jump up. Or someone would say something about selling, and pretty soon I was getting a vision to do it.

So when the opportunity came, I went to work for a new and used car dealership that two Christian friends of mine were managing for the owner. I can't say I was the best salesman, but it seems that God had me there to be a witness for Him and to learn. They had the idea of putting New Testament Bibles in each of the glove boxes, and so many times it would create an opportunity to share the gospel.

One such time was when a newly married couple came in to buy a used car. We looked over the lot, and they saw one they wanted to take for a test drive. I went to get the keys, and the three of us got in the car. The wife was in the driver's seat since the car was to be for her. The husband was next to her, and I was in the back seat. As she was driving down the street, he opened up the glove box to look inside, and out fell the New Testament. He held it up and spoke to his wife, remarking about finding a Bible in the glove box. I said the dealership had placed it there and also in every car on the lot. She said, **"Are you a Christian?"** and I replied, **"Yes."** As we were driving, the husband turned to me and said, **"Do you believe in speaking in tongues?"** I was kind of surprised by the question but replied, **"Well, the Bible talks about it in Acts 2:4 and in 1 Corinthians chapter 12 as well as other** places." He said, **"Yea, that's what I thought, but how come no one in our church does?"** I said, "What kind of church do you go to?" and he replied, "A Nazarene church." I said, **"I have a friend who went to one, and he speaks in tongues. I bet there are some in your church also. You just haven't met them yet.** They probably do it in prayer meetings on weeknights in the basement" (wondering why I said it that way). So from the time we drove until the time we got back to the dealership, they asked me questions about the gifts of the Spirit and other issues.

Later we were sitting at my desk trying to work up a deal on this car when I sensed in my spirit that we shouldn't be doing this. I said, **"You know, you two aren't here to buy a car today! I mean I'll sell you a car if you want, but I believe God brought you both here for another reason."** "Why are we here?" he said. **"You are here to receive the baptism in the Holy Spirit. Would you like to do that?"** **"Yes,"** they said with excitement, and I said, "Follow me." I walked into the sales manager's office, and I told him I had a couple who needed to be filled with the Holy Spirit, and he smiled and said, "Great, take them into the back office." So we headed to the back room, and once we were there, I gave them a little instruction on receiving the Spirit's power.

Just as I was about to pray, this young man closed his eyes and raised his hands and started singing an old gospel song, **"The comforter has come, the Comforter has come!"** And guess what? He came and filled them both! When they opened their eyes, their countenance looked as if they were seeing for the very first time. **"Everything looks different,"** he remarked, looking around the room as if seeing into another land. The presence of the Lord was strong as God filled them both with His power.

We just stood in His presence for a while, and then they left with great joy in their hearts. About four months later, I was walking in a shopping mall with my wife when I heard someone call my name, "Greg! Greg!" I turned around and looked to see the same couple from the dealership walking up to me. The first thing he said was, "You were right, there are people in the basement speaking in tongues during the weeknights!"

God is good!

> And they will lay hands on the sick, and they will recover.
>
> Mark 16:18

Working new car sales involves spending a lot of time waiting or working previous customers by phone. One time while I was waiting, a gentleman came into the showroom wearing what looked like a pair of coke bottles for glasses. They were very thick lenses. He told me that his eye doctor said he would probably be legally blind in a year or less. He had never owned a new car, and so he wanted to buy one before he could no longer see to drive. I told him I would be glad to sell him a car but also that I was a Christian and believed in the power of prayer. I asked him if he believed God could heal his eyes, and he said, **"Yes, I believe God could do that."** I said, **"Sir, you have great faith. Could I pray for you?"** I placed my hands on him and prayed a simple prayer for the Lord to heal his eyes.

Nothing in the natural seemed to happen immediately, but I have learned to pray the prayer of faith and not to doubt if circumstances or things do not change right away. We tried to find him a car, but there was nothing on the lot he liked, so he eventually left, unable to find what he wanted. The next day was my day off, but when I went back to work on the following day, I was told by another salesman that this man had come in to leave me a message that he had been healed and no longer needed his glasses. Praise God! Jesus is the same yesterday, today, and forever!

Personally, I found witnessing to people to come easier for me than selling cars, but the Lord continued to use the experience to change me and work His will in my life. As time went on, several people got saved, and some, like the man with the glasses, were healed. Eventually, I began sensing the Holy Spirit leading me into a different type of selling experience—one that would continue to challenge me and bring about more fruit and change into my life.

> But the people that do know their God shall
> be strong, and do exploits.
>
> Daniel 11:32

> The wicked flee when no man pursueth: but
> the righteous are bold as a lion.
>
> Proverbs 28:1

I believe God has meant the Christian life to be a great adventure. Even though we live in perilous times, and wicked men seem to be growing worse and worse, God wants us to know we are secure in Him and He will grant us the boldness we need as we trust in Him. We need to understand that the non-Christian is ruled by fear, while the believer is to walk in faith and love and discipline.

> For God hath not given us the spirit of fear;
> but of power, and of love, and of a sound
> mind.
>
> 2 Timothy 1:7

The apostle Paul writes in 1 Peter 3:13-15, "And who is he that will harm you, if ye be followers of that which is good? But and if ye suffer for righteousness' sake, happy are ye: and be not afraid of their terror, neither be troubled; but sanctify the Lord God in your hearts: and be ready always to give an answer to every man that asketh you a reason of the hope that is in you with meekness and fear" (King James Version).

The New American Standard Bible translates verse 14 like this: "AND DO NOT **FEAR** THEIR **INTIMIDATION, AND DO NOT BE TROUBLED**" (emphasis mine).

The words "fear" and "intimidation" are both translated from the Greek word *phobas*. You could translate it, Don't fear their fear! It's the word we get "phobia" from. For instance, if you have the fear of flying or the fear of spiders, you have a phobia. What the Holy Spirit is saying here is, Don't have a phobia about their phobia. Don't receive the fear that they live under into your heart. Because as Proverbs 29:25 warns us, "The fear of man brings a snare, but he who trusts in the LORD will be exalted" (NASB).

Verse 13 of 1 Peter 3 says, "And who is he that will harm you, if ye be followers of that which is good?" (KJV).

The word "harm" in verse 13 is the Greek word *Kakos*. It's the word Jesus used to describe evil spirits. He said they were *Kakos* spirits, or spirits of wickedness. So the Holy Spirit is giving us insight through the apostle Peter that persecution is demonic in origin. There is something behind people who are persecuting you. They are coming with *Kakos* intentions, evil intentions. The devil wants you to back off of your commitment to Christ and to back off of the boldness. Don't do it. I had one man say to me, **"If you mention the name of Jesus to me one more time, I will punch you in the face."** I replied, **"Sir, I am not trying to make you angry. If you don't want to hear about Jesus, may I tell you about the apostle Paul?"**

Now I know we don't want to be intentionally obnoxious or try to invite persecution, but if we remember what Paul said in Ephesians 6:12, "that we wrestle not against flesh and blood but against unseen forces," we will not lose heart, but preach the Word in love. If God be for us, who can be against us? Sharing your faith is a great adventure, and Jesus is with us.

For I will not presume to speak of anything except what Christ has accomplished through me, resulting in the obedience of the Gentiles by word and deed, in the power of signs and wonders, in the power of the Spirit; so that from Jerusalem and round about as far as Illyricum I have fully preached the gospel of Christ.

Romans 15:18-19

But he who boasts, let him boast in the Lord.

2 Corinthians 10:17

Story Thirteen: **Adman for Jesus**

The mind of man plans his way, but the LORD directs his steps.

Proverbs 16:9

The next job the Lord led me to was selling advertising for a firm that had a contract with a large chain of grocery stores. After my training, I was traveling to different cities to work the stores. My experiences in selling cars had given me more experience and confidence in talking to people, and I was excited to be on the road anticipating what the Lord might do.

I drove into the town of Port Townsend on the peninsula of Washington state, and the first thing I did was go to a pay phone and call my wife to let her know I had arrived safely. She told me she had a dream the previous night and saw me next to a boat or a ship and that she felt I was to find someone who had a boat or who was building a boat. I looked out of the pay phone booth toward the dock of the bay and gazed at a dozen or more boats tied up to the pier. "There are a lot of boats here," I said. "Well," she said, **"I just think there is someone God wants you to talk to who has a boat."**

After I hung up, I got in my car, praying for the Lord to direct me, standing on the promise in Romans 8:14: "For as many as are led by the Spirit of God, they are the sons of God." I drove through the town and came to the other end, then drove around a building located on the beach and stopped by a charter boat business. I looked at the sign on the building, thinking that this business might be a good prospect to sell advertising to, so I went inside looking for the owner. There was an older man in the office, and I asked him if the owner was in. He said that the owner was downtown in the old post office and city building on the third or fourth floor.

I thanked him, drove to the location, and asked someone in the lobby where I might find this gentleman. After getting more directions, I made my way up to the floor where his office was located. It was a very large, turn-of-the-century building, with big hallways, tall ceilings, lots of wood molding with some old brass. I knocked on the door, and a man I presumed to be in his late twenties answered. I introduced myself and asked if I could talk to him about some unique advertising for his business. He invited me in, and I looked around the room, spotting a drafting table and an artist's drawing of a small ship, or passenger ferry, above it. I asked what he was doing. He said he was in the process of designing a new ferry boat for commuters. I remembered my wife's dream, thinking, *Is this him?* He also said he was into shipping fresh fruit in decorative boxes.

He went into another room to get me a sample, so while he was gone, I walked over to a book shelf and spotted an older book on the Holy Spirit called *Nine O'clock in the Morning*, by Dennis Bennett. God used this man to bring the Holy Spirit's baptism and renewal to many. I mentioned it to him when he came back into the room, and He said with real interest, **"Do you know about the Holy Spirit?"** I said, **"Yes."** He got real excited and started to tell me of how he was in a church in the Seattle area visiting with a friend and how on that particular Sunday, there was a guest minister speaking.

The minister called him out during the service and said at a given time yet to come he will have a man come to him and tell him about the baptism in the Holy Spirit, and the man will pray for him. I got excited knowing this was the guy in the dream and why I was there. I told him the story, and we both got excited knowing God had arranged our meeting. We joined together in prayer, as I asked Jesus to baptize him in the Holy Spirit and with power. He received the Holy Spirit, and after rejoicing in the Lord and spending time in fellowship, I blessed him and left to continue working. I remember how hard it was to do anything the rest of the day without talking about Jesus. What an adventure it is to serve the Lord. In the world, there are so many people living lives that seem meaningless, and so they find their excitement in so many temporal and unrewarding ways, yet Jesus has come that we might have life and have it more abundantly.

I believe one of the reasons many people are not happy in their work or the reason people feel unfulfilled is because they do not approach their jobs with an understanding that it is a gift from God and a mission field, a place to serve the Lord.

I love the passage in Ecclesiastes 5:18-20: "Behold, that which I have seen to be good and to be comely is for one to eat and to drink, and to enjoy good in all his labor, wherein he laboreth under the sun, all the days of his life which God hath given him: for this is his portion. Every man also to whom God hath given riches and wealth, and hath given him power to eat thereof, and to take his portion, and to rejoice in his labor—this is the gift of God. For he shall not much remember the days of his life; because God answereth him in the joy of his heart." Work is not just to put food on the table, although as Scripture says, we need to work and provide for our families, but it also gives us the opportunity to fulfill our destiny and be salt and light. Jesus did not come to be served, but to serve. He is our example. Our time at work can become a time where we allow the love of God to flow through us to serve those we work with in the Spirit of Christ. Many in the world serve others out of selfishness, by only doing a good job when they know someone is watching over their shoulder. As Christians, Colossians admonishes us to "obey in everything those who are your earthly masters, not with eye service, as men-pleasers, but in singleness of heart, fearing the Lord. Whatever your task, work heartily, as serving the Lord and not men, knowing that from the Lord you will receive the inheritance as your reward; you are serving the Lord Christ" (Colossians 3:22-24).

Work can be more than just a responsibility; it can be an opportunity to serve the Lord by serving others, thereby giving us purpose and filling our hearts with joy. Work is a great place to build relationships with the pre-Christian, trusting the Holy Spirit to give you the grace and wisdom, along with revelation, on how to reach them for Christ.

It's Not Strange, but True: There's Glory in You!

> *To such an extent that they even carried the sick out into the streets, and laid them on cots and pallets, so that when Peter came by, at least his shadow might fall on any one of them.*
>
> *Acts 5:15*

After ministering to the boat builder, I began making my rounds with the local businesses, looking to make a sale. I noticed a Christian bookstore and decided to go in and talk to them. When I walked through the door, I greeted the salesman working the floor, who, for some reason, seemed to be looking at me intently. I excused myself and went back out to my car to get some material. When I returned to talk to him, he had a startled look on his face. He said, **"Could I ask you a question?"** I replied, **"Sure."** He said, **"Just before you walked in here the first time, I had been suffering all day with a head cold, and I was feeling pretty sick. When you walked in, all my symptoms went away, and when you walked out, they all came back. Now you're back, and they are gone. Can you tell me what is going on?"** I told him it wasn't me, but the presence of the Lord. I said, **"I'm a Christian, and the presence of the Lord is manifesting here."** I suggested we pray and ask the Lord to heal him. He agreed, and I prayed, commanding the sickness

54

to go in the name of Jesus. The Lord brought healing to his body, and we both rejoiced at the goodness of God.

Later on I read in Acts about Peter's shadow. Well, it wasn't his shadow that was healing people, but the glory of the Lord that was on Peter as he walked down the street. Paul tells us, "It's Christ in you, the hope of glory." I really believe as God continues to increase His glory on the church, we will see more and more of this type of demonstration of His goodness.

> To whom God would make known what is the riches of the glory of this mystery among the Gentiles; which is Christ in you, the hope of glory.
>
> Colossians 1:27

What a great adventure the Lord was giving me here in this small peninsula town. Even though I was doing well with the advertising and would be finishing up soon, the greatest satisfaction for me was being used of God to share the hope of the gospel to a few here and there.

I decided to look in at a small gift shop and find a gift to take home to my wife. While I was in the store browsing, I felt a tug in my spirit toward the lady who was sitting at the cash register near the front of the store. I asked the Lord if He had a word for this lady or something I could say to her, and this Scripture in Philippians came to my mind: "And my God will supply all your needs according to His riches in glory in Christ Jesus" (Philippians 4:19).

I have to admit that I actually told the Lord I already knew that one and asked if He could give me something else for her. I was questioning, Was this me or the Holy Spirit? Nothing else came to my mind, and it wouldn't go away. So as I was leaving, I said, **"Excuse me, I am a Christian, and I believe God wants you to know that He says in Philippians 4:19, 'And my God will supply all your needs according**

to His riches in glory in Christ Jesus.' " She looked at me real seriously, like she had never heard that before, and said, "Could you say that again?" "Sure," I replied. **"And my God will supply all your needs according to His riches in glory in Christ Jesus."** Now with tears in her eyes, she said, **"Would you please repeat that for me?"** **"And my God will supply all your needs according to His riches in glory in Christ Jesus,"** I replied the third time. Wiping the tears from her eyes, she began to tell me of how she had woken up that morning and taken a look at the bills and money she owed and wondered how she could continue to keep the store open. She prayed, asking God for help and direction. The Lord had answered, and this lady had faith to trust Him for her needs. Thank you, Jesus!

You know, not only do unbelievers need to be witnessed to, but so do many Christians who may feel as if they are in a desert, or maybe they just need a word of encouragement. In church many Christians want to prophesy and be used of God in the services. This is good and scriptural since we are to desire spiritual gifts and exercise them.

> Pursue love, yet desire earnestly spiritual gifts, but especially that you may prophesy.
> 1 Corinthians 14:1

I am all for prophecy in the local church to build up the body, but how about going outside the four walls of the church and looking to the hurting and discouraged and beginning to exhort, comfort, and edify them with the Word of the Lord. I know, you probably won't be recognized or have anyone pat you on the back and say, "Well done, thou mighty prophet of God," but God will be pleased with your unselfish demonstration of love. We could spend the rest of our lives encouraging people in this world we live in.

Proverbs 25:11 says, "A word fitly spoken is like apples of gold in pictures of silver."

I was thankful to the Lord for the word He gave me to give to this lady, but at the same time, I was aware I nearly missed God by thinking she needed something more spectacular. God knows better than I do what each person needs to hear at the present time. *Lord, help me not to lean on my own understanding, but to trust You and be obedient.*

From time to time, we all need to be encouraged, especially in the things we do day in and day out. Outside sales did not always come easy for me, but God is faithful to encourage us as we humble ourselves and look to Him. On one particular occasion, I was not having a very good week, and I was getting a little discouraged. It seemed that each business door I knocked on was shut in my face. I was standing outside my vehicle in the shade of the noon day, feeling like I should just call it quits. I decided I needed a Word from the Lord, so I opened up my Bible, and my eyes fell on this verse: "Be timid in business and come to beggary; be bold and make a fortune" (Proverbs 11:16b NEB).

Wow! That blew the discouragement right out the door! Isn't God amazing? Armed with a Word that brought faith, I repented of fear and timidity and continued to work. I think it was the second door that opened when a sale was finally made. What would have happened if I had allowed the discouragement to remain? I may have ended up defeated and quit, but the Father is faithful to give us what we need as we look not to ourselves or even our inadequacies but look unto Him, Who is the Author and Finisher of our faith.

Story Fourteen: **Ragman for Jesus**

Selling advertising took me away from home a lot, and so I began to pray about finding something where I could work locally and stay closer to home. One of the guys I had befriended at the ad agency was leaving to go to work for another company. He was taking on the lead sales position, and since they were looking for another salesman, he asked me to consider it. It would mean selling close to home, so after praying about it and meeting with the owner, I took the job.

My new job was selling industrial wipes; I became a ragman by trade. Not exactly your most prestigious or exciting vocation, but then God had led me to take it, and working with Him is always a blessing and exciting. After about a week into the job and learning the territory, I entered a little storefront business in downtown Renton. As I walked into the shop, I noticed the slogan on the wall: "Give the Gift of Life; Give a Job." It was a small janitorial referral company. A lady came out and asked me how she could help me. I introduced myself and asked her if I could see the owner. She left, and soon a stout man came out and said, "May I help you?" I shared what I had to offer and asked if he had any need for these items. He led me back to his supply room, and I saw we could provide him with the same product at a better price, so we went to his desk and began to discuss a deal.

I felt the prompting of the Holy Spirit that He wanted me to witness to this owner. *Now? Here in front of his secretary?* I thought, looking at this lady who was eyeballing me. *What if she throws me out?* The Holy Spirit continued to nudge me. He handed me a brochure with the statement **"Give the Gift of Life; Give a Job."** He told me about the many young people and underprivileged people he had placed into the work force by first training them and then seeing them placed into a job. I commended him for his vision and desire to help others. I then told him that his brochure reminded me of someone else who gave the gift of life by giving **His life**. I began to tell him of Jesus, pausing at times to let him respond. He said he was raised in church but was no longer attending and had not since he was a small boy. I asked him, **"Why?"** He began to tell me a very sad story. **"When I was a young boy, when I was on my way home from school, I decided to cut across the lawn of a corner house, and when I did, a man came out yelling at me to get off his grass. The man was the pastor of the church I had just started attending. Feeling humiliated and hurt, I never went back to that church."** My heart sank as he told me this story. I felt the love of God rise up in me as I began to tell him how sorry I was that he had been spoken to that way, especially by a pastor. I told him even though the man was wrong to react that way, we need to guard our hearts lest a root of bitterness come in and we are defiled. Offenses are a trap the devil uses to take us out of the way by getting us to be angry and, eventually, bitter at man or God. It's important to know that while we may be one hundred percent innocent of the abusive treatment we receive from individuals, we are one hundred percent responsible for our reaction toward them. Jesus said, "Father, forgive them; they don't know what they are doing."

> See to it that no one comes short of the grace
> of God; that no root of bitterness springing up
> causes trouble, and by it many be defiled.
> Hebrews 12:15

Bitterness can come as a result of real or supposed real treatment. It doesn't matter which. I shared with him that God wanted him to forgive that pastor because if he did not forgive him, then his Father in heaven would not forgive him. That is the truth of God's Word, and even though it may be difficult for some to hear, we are called to speak the truth in love. I shared this with him in a non-condemning tone. My desire was to see him restored unto the Lord.

> "For if you forgive men for their transgressions, your heavenly Father will also forgive you. But if you do not forgive men, then your Father will not forgive your transgressions."
> Matthew 6:14-15

After I shared these Scriptures with him, he admitted he needed to forgive. I invited him to pray and forgive the man and then to ask God for forgiveness. I then said, **"Why don't we kneel right here and pray?"** To be honest, I don't usually ask people to kneel, especially someone in front of his employees, but there was such a strong presence of the Holy Spirit at that moment that it seemed like the right thing to do. The man got out in front of his desk, and we both knelt to pray. I remember glancing over to my left and seeing his secretary continue to work like we were not even there! The phone rang, and she answered it, but this man kneeling didn't even seem to notice. God was healing his heart.

I led him in a prayer of forgiveness toward the pastor who spoke angrily at him when he was a youth, and then he asked God to forgive him for allowing bitterness to have a place in his heart. He then gave his life completely over to the Lordship of Christ and was set free from his sin and the hurts of the past. To God be the glory! He is so good. I left not with a sale, but with something much greater and of more value: the joy of seeing the Father restore a man to Him. It always amazes me how people will open up to God when the Holy Spirit is working. We always tend to think people will reject us or get angry. Sometimes this does happen, but they are not rejecting us, but the Father Who has sent us. When a person does yield to the work of the Holy Spirit, it is so wonderful. God will be faithful to bless us and meet our needs as He did mine as we continue to seek first His kingdom.

Story Fifteen: **Prince of Peace, Not Piece**

Peace I leave with you; My peace I give to
you; not as the world gives, do I give to you.
Let not your heart be troubled, nor let it be
fearful.

John 14:27

It was early morning when a guy walked into the office
looking kind of rugged with brown stringy hair. He asked if
anyone had jumper cables to jump-start his pickup. I said I
did and went out to my car. He said he was right across the
street, partway up the alley. I told him I would get my cables
and walk on over. I brought him the cables, and he hooked
up one side to his truck and the other end to the battery of
a car parked in the stall by the truck. After the jump, he
thanked me and started to get in the truck. I felt the Holy
Spirit's prompting and said, **"You know, life can be like a
car battery—sometimes we can use a good jump-start. I
have found Jesus to be a great Source of power. He has
power to give life. As a matter of fact, He said He came
that we might have life and have it more abundantly. He
also gave us a peace in a world where there is none to be
found."**

The guy in the car looked at me funny and then reached
over to his glove box and pulled out a hand gun, held it up
and said, **"This is my piece. It's all I need and goes with
me everywhere." "Yes,"** I replied, **"but it doesn't last, and
it won't take away the fear. Besides, those who live by the
sword die by the sword, and those who live by the gun die
by the gun. Only Jesus can take away the fear. Jesus said,
My peace I give to you, not as the world gives do I give it
to you."** The man looked at me and replied, **"What time are
your church services on Sunday?"**

God has placed within every individual the knowledge of His existence. Sometimes it just takes a little straight talk to help people say what they sometimes are hesitant to admit. They really do need God.

Story Sixteen: **Airline and Airport Stories**

After selling in different jobs for a few years, I started desiring a job where I could work at night and devote my daytimes to transitioning into full-time ministry within a local church where God had placed me. This is what I felt to be the leading of the Lord. I prayed and asked the Lord to give me a night job of some kind, and then I mentioned in the prayer that I wanted to be able to fly my family to Disneyland, too. This may seem funny, but it was a desire of my heart. Several weeks later, I ran into a Christian brother at a gym who told me of a major airline company that was hiring but was having trouble getting enough people who could pass the drug test. I went in, filled out an application, took the drug test, and soon was hired to work in the Cabin Service Department on the night shift. After working there a short time, I was given a free pass for my family, and we all flew to Disneyland. God is good!

Working for the airline afforded my wife and me to do a little bit of traveling. Using one of our free passes, we took a flight headed for Minnesota to attend a Christian conference. We were sitting in the first-class section. The airline companies would place their employees, non-revenue passengers, in any available seats. There were two empty aisle seats in the first-class section, so we were placed there. My wife was sitting next to me across the aisle, and sitting to my left was a woman reading a novel.

After a time of travel, I heard the Holy Spirit speak to me to talk to this woman. I turned and asked her what she was reading. She kind of blushed and said, **"Oh, just some romance novel."** I laughed a little, acknowledging her embarrassment, and then said, **"Have you ever read John 3:16?"** She replied, **"No—what's it about?"** **"It's about the greatest love story ever told,"** I said, and pulled my New Testament Bible out of my pocket and turned to the

Gospel of John and read to her the Bible verse. To my relief, instead of being turned off, she became greatly interested and told me she had begun to read the Bible to her child every evening at bedtime. I asked her if she went to church, and she said no, but she had some friends up in Canada who belonged to some kind of non-denominational church that was very "lively and outgoing," as she put it. I knew from her description these friends had probably witnessed to her and were praying for her, so I began directing the conversation toward the plan of salvation. After answering a few of the questions she had about God and the Bible, I began to share what it meant to be born again. Eventually, I asked her if there was any reason why she couldn't receive Jesus Christ into her life right then, and to my joy, she agreed to receive Jesus. We joined hands, and I led her in a short prayer of repentance and confession to receive Jesus, and then prayed for her and her child. The rest of the flight, I sort of gave her a Bible study on what to do now that she was a Christian and how to continue to grow in grace. I also told her to contact her friends in Canada when she got home and to let them know of her conversion.

This was a good example of someone planting seeds and praying, and then another coming along and reaping where they had not sown. This lady who sat next to me was a nurse and was ready and prepared by the Holy Spirit to receive eternal life. My wife and I rejoiced as God had given us another divine appointment. I believe God many times sets us up to be in just the right place at the right time. If we will understand this and expect miracles, we will see God move.

After the trip, I was back at work, where God gave me favor, and eventually, after a time, I was given a lead position on the graveyard shift. This worked out real well, giving me the freedom I needed during the day. At night we worked in a team of five. One of my team members, a Christian man, was leaving the company to work elsewhere. I was sorry to see him go because I had enjoyed the fellowship and encouragement since I was the only Christian in that particular department. I had been doing a lot of witnessing as the opportunities arose, but it had been a hard field to evangelize.

After he left, I began to pray for the Lord to send me another Christian worker to work alongside me. When I came to work one evening, the boss called me into the office to introduce me to my new co-worker, whom I would be training. I walked in and met a young man, who greeted me, and immediately, I discerned he was a homosexual. He was openly gay and let everyone know it. I have to admit, when I left the office and was alone, I turned to the Lord and really whined about why I had to get him for a co-worker. "Well," I said to myself, "I'll just have to make the best of it."

Of course, my attitude toward him was not exactly an example of Christian love, but this guy was really out of the closet and in your face. God has a way of showing you what's on the inside of you. It can be very humbling, but needed if we are to be His ambassadors. The Lord began to really work on my heart concerning this gay guy. I was about to learn some things.

I was in a truck with two other workers, driving across the tarmac, when the driver of the truck started in on this gay guy and his inability to grasp certain simple job assignments given. They began to use a name for describing him, like queer and fag. The next thing I knew, the word "queer" came out of my mouth, and as soon as it did, I got this strong rebuke from the Holy Spirit, saying, **"Do not call him that word again."** I was really taken aback, not so much by the rebuke as by the sudden revelation that I was falling into a trap of the enemy to label a sinner who needed Christ in a category apart from any other lost person. By taking on this attitude along with the rest of the workers, I was distancing myself from being used of God to be salt and light and to speak the truth in love.

Homosexuality is a sin, and such behavior is clearly unbiblical, but to label that person with a degrading name in my opinion is counterproductive to the Spirit of Christ. I realize many gay people even use these terms to describe themselves, but God was calling me to a higher place. I repented and started to pray for him. I thought I was doing well until one day, he came up to me and invited me to go to lunch with him. We had an hour for lunch, and most of the workers usually went to Denny's across from the airport because it was close and open for twenty-four hours. I looked at him, and all I could think of was sitting in this restaurant and everyone there seeing me with this gay guy. I politely made some excuse and said, "No, thanks," and he walked away. He no sooner had left when the Holy Spirit convicted me of my hypocrisy. **"Jesus ate with sinners; are you greater than He? Why are you so worried about your reputation when Jesus made Himself of no reputation?"** God sure has a way of getting your attention. I felt really bad and immediately repented and promised the Lord I would invite him to lunch the next day.

When the next day came, I asked him to lunch, and he gladly accepted. We went to the restaurant, and as we sat there talking, he asked me how I became a Christian. It really surprised me, but I should have known. I should have believed God. So I gave him my testimony, and he listened intently. He thanked me for sharing, and after our lunch, we went back to work. My heart was changing for this guy. I was sensing the love of God for him growing in me. I continued to pray, and I made it a point to be his friend. I even found myself defending him when the other workers made their sarcastic and, at times, hateful comments.

One night while working on an airplane, he came up to me and asked my permission to leave the plane and use the restroom in the terminal. I said sure, and as he left, the Holy Spirit said to me, **"He has gone to purge himself."** I said, **"What?"** because I wasn't sure what purge meant. And the Holy Spirit said plainly, **"He went to vomit."** The Lord explained that, as a homosexual, he was obsessed by his weight and would often use purging to keep his weight down and that it was something that he could not control. When he came back to the plane, his appearance was very pale, and there were beads of sweat on his forehead.

I waited on the Lord for direction, and the Holy Spirit directed me to speak to him about it. I said, **"I know why you went to the restroom."** He said, **"You do?"** and I said, **"You went to purge and get rid of your meal."** He looked at me and said, **"How did you know?"** I said, **"The Holy Spirit told me."** He had a look of despair and replied that he had been doing it for years and couldn't stop. I told him that God understood and that the Lord could heal him of this if he would let Him. He asked me if he would have to give up his lifestyle. I said God was willing to heal him, but the sin of homosexuality came with much bondage that would only be broken permanently by completely turning away from it and turning to Jesus, trusting Him to do the work. He wanted to think about it. I told him not to wait very long because when God is speaking to your heart, it isn't wise to harden it. From that moment on, he began to open up and talk to me about personal things.

He shared many things with me, being his friend. One day he told me what led him into the homosexual lifestyle. He told me he was sexually taken advantage of by a youth pastor at a camp retreat. He struggled with his sexual identity for years before giving in to the lie that he must be a homosexual. Naturally, his trust for ministers and Christians in general was not very good. This incident eventually took him to look to the gay community for acceptance and identity. He continued to struggle with the decision to come to Christ. I continued to pray and be his friend. In fact, sometimes it seemed like I was the only one there who treated him with any respect. Things didn't go too well for him with the other workers, and he was always sick. His work performance went downhill, and eventually, he transferred to another department in another city in order to keep his job with the airline. The day he left he came to me to say goodbye and to thank me for being a friend. I told him God loved him and wanted to set him free. I would continue to pray for him. I never saw him again.

There is a real need to reach out to those bound by sexual sins. It can be a real challenge, but God can give us the wisdom and grace to do it. I also believe the church will see an increase in persecution come from the gay activists, who will continue to press their agenda. We must be careful not to respond as the disciples did in asking the Lord to send fire down from heaven when the people did not receive the words of Christ. I like what one pastor remarked when questioned about his Christian response toward the homosexuals who had stormed his church one Sunday and shouted down anyone who tried to speak from the pulpit and then littered his home with pro-gay material and signs. His response was, **"I could no more be angry at them than I could be angry at a blind man for stepping on my foot."**

I learned a lot about working with homosexuals, and I believe the church has a lot to learn about the Christian response to the homosexual community. May the Lord give us wisdom and compassion to lead them to Christ. We cannot condone their sin, but we must see them for what they are— lost souls in need of God's forgiveness and Jesus as their Savior and Deliverer.

Mind-blinding Spirits

> But if our gospel be hid, it is hid to them that are lost: In whom the god of this world hath blinded the minds of them which believe not, lest the light of the glorious gospel of Christ, who is the image of God, should shine unto them.
>
> 2 Corinthians 4:3-4

This text in 2 Corinthians shows us that the god of this world, the devil, has blinded the minds of the lost. We need to bind the enemy from keeping the ones we are ministering the gospel to from seeing the light. We need to loose the light of the gospel of Christ upon them so they can see and turn to God. Satan is the deceiver; he has deceived many into a false security of living from day to day without any knowledge that judgment awaits all who refuse to accept the sacrifice of Christ and the cleansing of His shed blood.

The Lord demonstrated to me the truth of this passage as I was witnessing to a young woman at work one day. This Jewish woman was told by her parents growing up never to listen to Christians talk about Jesus. She wouldn't accept any New Testament Scriptures, but thank God, there are plenty of Old Testament prophecies concerning the Messiah. I asked her one day if I could show her in the Old Testament a wonderful reference to Jesus and His work on the cross, but before that, I asked her if I could pray for her. She agreed, and I simply prayed a quiet prayer in front of her, taking authority over the mind-blinding spirit, and I asked the Holy Spirit to reveal to her the truth about Christ. I then turned to Isaiah 53:1-11:

> Who hath believed our report? And to whom is the arm of the LORD revealed? For he shall grow up before him as a tender plant, and as a root out of a dry ground: he hath no form or comeliness; and when we shall see him, there is no beauty that we should desire him. He is despised and rejected of men; a man of sorrows, and acquainted with grief: and we hid as it were our faces from him; he was despised, and we esteemed him not. Surely he hath borne our griefs, and carried our sorrows: yet we did esteem him stricken, smitten of God, and afflicted. But he was

wounded for our transgressions; he was bruised for our iniquities: the chastisement of our peace was upon him; and with his stripes we are healed. All we like sheep have gone astray; we have turned every one to his own way; and the LORD hath laid on him the iniquity of us all. He was oppressed, and he was afflicted, yet he opened not his mouth: he is brought as a lamb to the slaughter, and as a sheep before her shearers is dumb, so he opened not his mouth. He was taken from prison and from judgment: and who shall declare his generation? For he was cut off out of the land of the living: for the transgression of my people was he stricken. And he made his grave with the wicked and with the rich in his death; because he had done no violence, neither was any deceit in his mouth. Yet it pleased the LORD to bruise him; he hath put him to grief: when thou shalt make his soul an offering for sin, he shall see his seed, he shall prolong his days, and the pleasure of the LORD shall prosper in his hand. He shall see of the travail of his soul, and shall be satisfied: by his knowledge shall my righteous servant justify many; for he shall bear their iniquities.

We read this together, and when we were done, I asked her who she thought the person described here could be, and she replied, "Jesus." After that we talked often about the Lord. She still needed to surrender her life to the Lordship of Christ, but the veil over her was being lifted so she could now be witnessed to effectively. She used to drive from Portland, Oregon, across the state line to Seattle every day to come to work—a four-hour drive from her house to the airport. One time as we were leaving work on the night shift, she looked really tired. I told her to be careful. As we left work, I followed her down to the freeway on-ramp, and as she headed south, I turned to go north. I asked the Lord to place angels around her car and to keep her awake and bring her safely home. The next day at work, she told me that she was halfway into her trip home when she fell asleep at the wheel. Then she heard what appeared to be a male voice yell, **"Wake up!"** She even remarked how it strangely sounded like me. Praise God for His ministering spirits, the angels, who are called to minister to those who shall be heirs of salvation.

> Are they not all ministering spirits, sent forth
> to minister for them who shall be heirs of
> salvation?
>   Hebrews 1:14

As we pray for the ones we are witnessing to, God will send His angels to continue to bring that word around to them again and again, putting them in situations to hear the spoken word or the gospel over and over again. Do not stop praying or believing for a friend or loved one.

While I was with this airline company, the Lord brought many opportunities to share Jesus. There was a young man who seemed to find it hard to make friends with the other workers. He was very talkative and, to some, seemed a little arrogant. He was raised Catholic, and we often would talk about Jesus and the Bible. He had many questions about what I thought the Bible meant on different subjects, and so I often would be able to share the Truth with him. One evening I noticed he seemed to be a little depressed. We were on an airplane working an overnight jet, so we had lots of time to talk while we worked. He was in the forward section of the plane, and when I came by, he said, "Do you think I will go to hell for causing a girl I once knew to have an abortion?"

He was genuinely convicted and concerned about his eternal destiny. He also asked me how long he would have to stay in purgatory. I told him that purgatory was not a biblical teaching and that the Bible clearly stated that for a Christian to be absent from the body is to be present with the Lord. For a non-Christian, Jesus told us about the rich man who died and opened his eyes in hell.

Elsewhere, the Bible says, "It is appointed unto man once to die and after that judgment" (Hebrews 9:27). I began to share with him that it isn't *just* this sin or that particular sin that sends a sinner to hell; rather, it is the sin of unbelief, not believing or trusting in Christ as your personal Savior. After sharing the gospel of grace with him, I asked him if he would like to receive Christ, and he said he would. Things began to change for him after that day, and one day he approached me to tell me that ever since he had invited Jesus into his heart, he had not had one migraine headache. Jesus *is* Savior and Healer!

Soon several of us began to meet and pray for the other workers. Word got around concerning our faith in Christ. We would meet at lunchtime and read the Word and encourage one another in the Lord.

> Preach the word; be ready in season and out
> of season; reprove, rebuke, exhort, with great
> patience and instruction.
> 2 Timothy 4:2

During my time working at the airport, I learned a lot about standing for the Lord. Especially when it seemed that the Good News I was sharing was falling on deaf ears. There were a few who called themselves Christians, but they were silent when it came to sharing their faith or defending the faith. I don't mean to be hard on those who were intimidated by the language and behavior of the ungodly. Many times I was reminded of what the Scripture says concerning Lot and his situation.

> And if He rescued righteous Lot, oppressed
> by the sensual conduct of unprincipled men
> (for by what he saw and heard that righteous
> man, while living among them, felt his
> righteous soul tormented day after day with
> their lawless deeds)
>
> 2 Peter 2:7-8

I, too, at times felt oppressed by the conduct of unprincipled men. Yet the Lord knows how to rescue the godly from temptation, and His grace is sufficient to keep us and to empower us to live for Him under such conditions. I have not yet sweated drops of blood as our Lord did in the time of His trial. The Lord was faithful to vindicate me and to show forth His power in unique ways. One night at work, another worker and I were in the service truck approaching a Lockheed L-1011, a large, wide-bodied jet that was in for overnight service. Three teams were assigned to work the aircraft. We were coming up to the middle door. Once we were in position, we got out of the cab, put the outriggers down to stabilize the truck, and walked to the rear of the truck and climbed in. We then began to lift the bed of the truck up approximately fifteen feet to the level of the passenger door.

The door to this aircraft is raised electronically, and it cannot be opened from the outside, unless it is first released on the inside and the emergency air slide is first disengaged. If you open the door before you disengage the air slide, you will deploy the large slide designed for emergency landings. This air slide is filled and thrust outward by large CO_2 gas canisters. If you get in the way, you could get seriously hurt, not to mention you have delayed a plane and all the passengers for quite some time. Once the truck was up and in position, we extended the hydraulic plank to walk out from the front of the truck bed to the door. As I looked toward the cabin windows, I saw one of the other workers walk down the aisle toward the door to open it. I was in front of my co-worker Johnny and ready to walk out toward the plane when I immediately heard the Holy Spirit say to me, **"Close the door,"** meaning pull down the door of the truck that was directly in front of us. I started to pull it down like you would a garage door, and my partner said, **"Why are you closing the door?"** I replied, **"Something is wrong."** Just as the door closed, we heard a loud boom as the air slide came out from the aircraft and rammed the truck. If we had been standing out on the plank like we usually did, we could have been knocked off the truck or crushed between the truck and the air slide by the force of it coming out.

Johnny looked at me with his eyes real big and said, **"How did you know that was going to happen?"** I replied, **"I heard the Holy Spirit tell me to close the door, and I knew when He said it something was not right."** Johnny, who was never given to praising the Lord, began to give shouts of thanks to God while grabbing me in the process. We used a ladder and climbed down the back of the truck. By this time, a small number of mechanics were staring at the scene and shaking their heads. This meant work for them and lots of paperwork and a delayed flight. Johnny and I went up the Jetway to the front of the plane to meet with the lead man in charge of the shift. As we walked in, Johnny began to point to me and tell everyone how God had told me to shut the door and how God had protected us from being hurt and that I was a good person to be next to in times of danger. It was kind of humorous listening to him go on and on about the matter. The foreman asked who opened the door, and everyone said her name.

The young lady who opened the door was a part-time employee and had slipped away in shame to hide; she was really shook up. She knew she had not just delayed a flight, but almost hurt two workers. Of course, it was an accident, but in the airline business, working carefully around expensive aircraft and the safety of others is a high priority.

She would be written up with some disciplinary action taken or terminated if she had any other write-ups. I was relieved they did not fire her. She was a good worker and just made a mistake. Word quickly got around about the incident, and the Lord received much glory. What the devil meant for evil, God turned around to open the hearts of the workers, giving me favor to share Christ. What made it interesting was the young lady who caused the incident was a Mormon who wasn't too keen on my witnessing. When I finally saw her, she was so humbled by the incident and relieved that I wasn't angry. She was taken aback that I was only concerned for her feelings. This created an opportunity to share with her about God's loving protection and forgiveness.

Story Seventeen: **Mad Dog**

There was a man at work who had earned the nickname "Mad Dog." The story goes that he had a difficult day at the ticket counter and, after handling the usual complaints, was confronted by a woman who was demanding that her small dog be allowed to have a seat next to her in the cabin. He was trying to explain to her unsuccessfully that her dog could not be in the cabin with the rest of the passengers, but in the area of the jet where the rest of the pets go. She continued to argue until he got so frustrated he actually got down on his hands and knees and crawled around the counter and nipped (but did not bite) the back of her heel. He says he mostly did it in fun in order to break the tension. He, of course, was reprimanded and demoted from the ticket counter. Because of this incident, he earned the nickname "Mad Dog," as well as a reputation for an employee who could go off the deep end anytime. Some of the workers stayed out of his way; others thought he was strange, but not dangerous. When he found out I was a Christian, he took a liking to me, and so whenever we were assigned work together, he would ask me questions about the Bible and we would talk about the things of God. He was raised in the church and even told me he, at one time, felt a call to pastor. I really believed that to be true and encouraged him that it was not too late. He had a lot of personal issues and found it hard to believe God would use him.

It is a sad truth that there are a lot of people like this man who, for one reason or another, have failed to appropriate the grace of God and yield all to Christ and serve Him fully. Many are called, but few are chosen. You really couldn't help but like Mad Dog. He was sort of a big teddy bear kind of guy who really did have a heart for helping people. Once he donated a large set of stadium risers and platform material he purchased at an auction to our church. We used them to build a stage and platform for the speaker and music team. One day he seriously hurt his back at work and had to go home and see a doctor. I began to pray for him and felt the Holy Spirit direct me to call him. I called him and asked him how he was. He said the doctor had taken x-rays and had told him it was serious and he may need surgery if it did not improve. I began to testify of how the Lord had healed my back years earlier when I worked at a cement company and that I wanted to share some Scriptures with him. I asked him if He had a Bible in the house, and he replied yes. I directed him to James 5:13-15, and then I read to him over the phone these verses:

> Is anyone among you suffering? Let him pray. Is anyone cheerful? Let him sing praises. Is anyone among you sick? Let him call for the elders of the church, and let them pray over him, anointing him with oil in the name of the Lord; and the prayer offered in faith will restore the one who is sick, and the Lord will raise him up, and if he has committed sins, they will be forgiven him (NASB).

Then I turned to the Gospel of Mark and read Mark 16:16-18:

> He who has believed and has been baptized shall be saved; but he who has disbelieved shall be condemned. And these signs will accompany those who have believed: in My name they will cast out demons, they will speak with new tongues; they will pick up serpents, and if they drink any deadly poison, it shall not hurt them; they will lay hands on the sick, and they will recover.

After reading these verses, I shared with him how Jesus healed the sick and made provision for us to receive healing through his death and resurrection. I read to him the words of Matthew 8:17: "In order that what was spoken through Isaiah the prophet might be fulfilled, saying, 'He Himself took our infirmities, and carried away our diseases.' " I then told him to listen to these words by the apostle John in 1 John 5:14: "And this is the confidence which we have before Him, that, if we ask anything according to His will, He hears us. And if we know that He hears us in whatever we ask, we know that we have the requests which we have asked from Him."

I said to him: **"God is telling us that if we ask anything according to His will, He will hear us, and we can have confidence in knowing, not only does He hear us, but we will have the answer to what we ask for if we ask according to His will!"** I told him that according to the Scriptures we just read, we can have confidence when we pray for healing for his back. I asked him if He believed God wanted to heal him, and he replied, "Yes." I asked him if I could come over and anoint him with oil and pray, and he told me to come. I got some oil, grabbed my Bible, and headed for his house. When I arrived at his house, I knocked on the door, and I heard him holler, **"Come in."** I opened the door and stepped in to find him resting on the couch. I asked him if he was ready to have prayer, and he replied, "Yes." I reminded him of the Scriptures we were standing on and took out the oil, put a drop on my finger, and applied it to his forehead. The presence of the Holy Spirit became strong, and so I began to speak to his back and the disks, commanding in Jesus' name for him to be healed. I asked him how he felt, and he said he felt much better and could even move more freely. He got really excited, and we spent some time fellowshipping and talking about the Lord. I left for home rejoicing in the goodness of God.

In order for him to come back to work, he needed a note from his doctor, so he went in and was examined and given a clean bill of health! He came back to work boldly telling others of what God had done. It was exciting to see his heart turn toward the Lord. The goodness of God does lead us to repentance.

> Or despisest thou the riches of his goodness and forbearance and longsuffering; not knowing that the goodness of God leadeth thee to repentance?
>
> Romans 2:4

> When a man's ways are pleasing to the LORD, He makes even his enemies to be at peace with him.
>
> Proverbs 16:7

The Lord knows how to turn the hearts of those who may oppose us when we are serving Him. A classic example is when God turned Paul's heart from a persecutor of the church to an apostle to the Gentiles, and the Holy Spirit used Paul to give us the great doctrines of righteousness, justification, faith, and grace. We need to trust God and boldly speak the truth in love to those who we may feel are the hardest to win to Christ. There were times on the job when the spirit of anti-Christ was so strong it was easy to be intimidated by it. The Holy Spirit spoke to me one day while I was discouraged by being under its influence.

> Now, gird up your loins, and arise, and speak to them all which I command you. Do not be dismayed before them, lest I dismay you before them.
>
> Jeremiah 1:17

Webster says this about being dismayed:
verb, transitive
> 1.To destroy the courage or resolution of by exciting dread or apprehension.
> 2.To cause to lose enthusiasm; disillusion.
> 3.To upset or alarm.

noun
> A sudden or complete loss of courage in the face of trouble or danger.

God does not want His people to lose their courage or enthusiasm, nor be intimidated by the spirit of anti-Christ or by any man or the devil. We need to remember the words of apostle Paul in Ephesians 6:12:

> For our struggle is not against flesh and blood, but against the rulers, against the powers, against the world forces of this darkness, against the spiritual forces of wickedness in the heavenly places.

The entrance of God's work gives light (Psalms 119:130), and as the light of these Scriptures came into my soul, I broke free of the oppression and continued to openly share Christ as the Holy Spirit led. The Lord did many exciting things as we saw souls saved and many healed while I was with the airline. Eventually, the Lord opened the door for me to leave, and I left to go on, in the great adventure of following Jesus.

Story Eighteen: **Which Way to the Strip Clubs?**

A friend and I had traveled from Seattle to Portland to attend a street minister's witnessing seminar. We were doing some sightseeing between meetings and had just parked the car. I was waiting for him to join me, and as we were about to cross the street to visit the city's conference center, some guy in a car with a young girl pulled up and hollered out his window, **"Hey, do you know where any good strip joints are?"** (I don't know why I attract these kinds of people; I hope it's the Lord). I said I didn't have any idea since I was new in town but that I knew someone who could give them a better time. **"Who is that?"** he asked. **"Jesus,"** I replied. **"You see, He came that you might have life and have it more abundantly"** (John 10:10). He said, "Where are you from?" as if he didn't hear my response, and I said, "Renton, Washington." He gave a surprised look and said he also was from that area. I said, **"Now, isn't that interesting that of all the people in this big city, you pull over and ask a preacher from the same area and state you live in such a question."** He said, **"Maybe I should talk to you."** He pulled the car from the side of the road into the parking garage where we where standing and began to ask a few spiritual questions. I kept noticing the nervousness of the young girl next to him.

This guy had been drinking a lot, and I didn't know if much of what I was saying was entering his heart, let alone his head, so I directed my attention to the young girl next to him in the car. She said she was raised in the church but wasn't living the kind of life she should and that she probably should change. They both continued to ask questions about the Lord and what it means to be a Christian. I spoke to them about having a relationship with Christ and being free from sin and walking in victory. I told them that our meeting was not by chance (it never is), and that the heavenly Father was calling them home. He asked where I went to church and said maybe he would try to come. Then he said they needed to go. I asked him if I could pray for them, and he said he could use all the help he could get (he needed it). I prayed out loud for them both, asking God to reveal Himself to them and for His protection on their lives. He thanked us and then slowly drove off down the street.

In witnessing to people, it is important to remember the principle in God's Word that some of us plant seeds, some water, but God is faithful to give the increase.

> I have planted, Apollos watered; but God gave the increase. So then neither is he that planteth any thing, neither he that watereth; but God that giveth the increase.
>
> 1Corinthians 3:6-7

Every time you speak God's Word under the anointing of the Holy Spirit, it is a very powerful thing.

> For as the rain cometh down, and the snow from heaven, and returneth not thither, but watereth the earth, and maketh it bring forth and bud, that it may give seed to the sower, and bread to the eater: So shall my word be that goeth forth out of my mouth: it shall not return unto me void, but it shall accomplish that which I please, and it shall prosper in the thing whereto I sent it.
>
> Isaiah 55:10-11

Don't ever feel or think it's a waste of time to share your faith because it is not. When I was in sales, we were told not to prejudge people concerning who we thought would or would not buy our product. In sharing your faith, your job is to be faithful to witness, leaving the results in God's hands. **Remember, success in witnessing is not bringing someone to the Lord. Success in witnessing is living out your Christian life, sharing the gospel, and trusting God for the results.**

Once while witnessing to a young man on the street, he stopped me in the midst of my sharing the gospel to tell me that as I was speaking, the words were physically striking him in the chest. He could actually feel something touching the area around his heart. I told him that Jesus said, **"My words, they are spirit and they are life"** (John 6:63). As we share our faith in Christ, God will take the words and cause them to have an impact on the hearts of the people. Whether or not people actually physically feel anything is not the point; the Word is a seed, and it will go to the heart. We do need to protect the seed with prayer, believing the Lord to water it and bring forth an increase.

> The sower soweth the word. And these are they by the way side, where the word is sown; but when they have heard, Satan cometh immediately, and taketh away the word that was sown in their hearts.
>
> Mark 4:14-15

In the parable of the sower, Jesus explained to His disciples that the seed was the Word, and when it was sown, it went to the heart, but that immediately, Satan comes to steal the Word that was sown in their hearts. The Word that you speak goes to the heart of man because that is what it is designed to do. We need to pray as well as continue to sow because the enemy wants to steal the Word of God.

Story Nineteen: **Hail Satan, No! Hail Jesus!**

I had just pulled up to the church parking lot when I noticed three young guys dressed in black leather with silver chains hanging around their necks and belts looking in the church window. As I stepped out of the car, they raised their hands toward the church and yelled, "Hail Satan!" I immediately yelled back, **"NO! HAIL JESUS!"**

They were startled and turned to walk away quickly. I followed, saying, **"Wait a minute, don't leave. What are you guys up to?"** (not really knowing what I was going to say next, only that there was an opportunity to share Jesus). As we walked together up the street, I just started sharing the gospel with them. They stopped, and one of them began making comments about what he had been told about God growing up. He was raised Jehovah's Witnesses, but was not actively involved in it. As we talked back and forth, I discerned the heart of one of the young men opening up to the Word of God. I began directing my words toward him because he was listening with more than his ears.

He suddenly stopped and said in a cocky tone, **"Can you prove to me there is a God?"** and before I could think about a proper reply, I said, **"Sure, give me your hand."** He did, and then I asked him his name. **"Shawn,"** he replied, looking at me, wondering what I was going to do. Looking into his eyes, I started praying, asking the Holy Spirit to come and touch him with the love of God. Shawn's eyes got kind of big, and then he closed them as if he were enjoying a warm shower. I just blessed him with the Word of God and prayer, then after a short time released his hand. It was a very holy time as the presence of the Lord lingered for a few minutes. He just stood there with his eyes closed, and then he slowly opened them and looked up at me. I said, **"Did you feel that, Shawn?"** and he said really slowly, "Yeessss!"

I said, "There is your proof, Shawn—the manifest

presence of the Lord." From that moment on, there was no resistance in sharing my faith. After a while, they said they had to be going but would come back and stop by the church after they finished taking their friend to his place of work. I really wasn't sure if I would see them again, but I just committed them to the Lord and said goodbye and headed for the church. A couple of hours later, two of them, Shawn and one of the other young teens, showed up at the church. They began to ask more questions about Jesus and then wanted to tell me about an experience they had the night before at a party.

They said there was a guy who said he was a Satanist, who pointed his finger and spoke to a pop bottle, and it just blew up! This really scared them, and since that incident, they had experienced many thoughts of suicide and were feeling very depressed. I told them that what they had seen the man do was just a demonic manifestation and that even though demons had some power to perform signs and wonders, Jesus had defeated the devil at Calvary. Jesus had all power and all authority, and He had delegated it to his church, the body of Christ. They wanted to know how they could be free from the depression and thoughts of suicide, and so I told them Jesus could set them free if they would turn from their sin and receive Jesus into their hearts, making Him Lord of their lives.

I led them both in prayer and then rebuked a spirit of suicide and torment from them. They left the church saying they would be back on Wednesday. When they came back, they told me that after leaving the church that night, they had tried for several minutes to think of thoughts of death but could not even dwell on them and they felt totally free. Praise God for the power in the blood and the name of Jesus.

We Have Good News to Tell!

> To wit, that God was in Christ, reconciling the world unto himself, not imputing their trespasses unto them; and hath committed unto us the word of reconciliation. Now then we are ambassadors for Christ, as though God did beseech you by us: we pray you in Christ's stead, be ye reconciled to God. For he hath made him to be sin for us, who knew no sin; that we might be made the righteousness of God in him.
>
> 2 Corinthians 5:19

Eugene H. Peterson puts it this way in *The Message* (Bible):

> God put the world square with himself through the Messiah, giving the world a fresh start by offering forgiveness of sins. God has given us the task of telling everyone what he is doing. We're Christ's representatives. God uses us to persuade men and women to drop their differences and enter into God's work of making things right between them. We're speaking for Christ himself now; become friends with God; he's already a friend with you.

The gospel is the Good News; it's called Good News because God isn't mad at you anymore. He poured out His wrath on His Son and placed your sins and mine on Jesus. He can justify you and I because He allowed Jesus to bear the penalty for us. Jesus willingly obeyed the Father, even to the point of dying on the cross, because He loves the Father and He loves you. Jesus paid the price to reconcile us to the

Father. All anyone in the world has to do is to turn from his or her sin, believe in Jesus, and receive God's forgiveness for sin. Nobody has to fear death and the consequence of being separated from God and their loved ones forever. Everyone can have eternal life if they will repent and believe in Jesus.

It is not just Good News; it's great news!

Eventually, the Lord opened the door for me to take a step of faith and leave the airline company I was working for and enter into full-time ministry serving at a local church in the town of Renton. God really blessed us there, and it was a great place to grow and serve the Lord. After several years of working in the church, we began to hear about a move of God taking place up in Toronto, Canada. The senior pastor, I, and another couple decided to fly to Toronto and visit the Airport Vineyard Church.

Story Twenty: **Fresh Oil and Fresh Fire**

God was definitely doing things at this little church by an airport. It was the first time I had ever come to a church service an hour and a half early and had to wait in line to get in. We stayed a week, attending each night to worship the Lord and to be prayed for at the end of each service during the ministry time. I remember lying on the floor after being prayed for, enjoying the peace and presence of the Lord, when my right arm started to shake. I began to wonder what God was doing, or if this was just me. I was thinking that I could probably stop this and get up, but I decided to yield, believing God was at work, and just see what would take place.

As I yielded my will to the Holy Spirit, my arm and both my legs started to shake. I know this sounds funny, but it felt as if my body were wrapped in gelatin or I had lots of fat on my limbs, and as I shook I could feel this substance around me. I wondered, *What is this?* and the Holy Spirit said to me, **"This is the anointing."** Then I recalled this scripture in Isaiah 10:27:

> So it will be in that day, that his burden will be removed from your shoulders and his yoke from your neck, and the yoke will be broken because of fatness.

> They shall be abundantly satisfied with the fatness of thy house; and thou shalt make them drink of the river of thy pleasures.
> Psalms 36:8

This fatness I was feeling was a manifestation of the anointing upon me, and my soul was "drinking from the river of His pleasures." After a while, it subsided, and when

I got up, I felt really refreshed in my spirit and renewed to serve the Lord. I didn't experience initially any laughter like a lot of people there did, but then I hadn't been outside the church in public yet, either. That came later as we left the church and waves of Holy Spirit joy filled our souls.

I believe the main reason for the infilling of the Holy Spirit is to receive power to effect the world for Christ, to receive power to be witnesses. I remembered what had happened to me years earlier as a new Christian when the Holy Spirit had first baptized me and I left the four walls of a church to go outside. The baptism in the Holy Spirit is not just a one-time experience. Paul writes in Ephesians 5:11, **"Be filled with the Spirit."** Filled here refers to a continuous process of being filled to overflowing.

When we left the service, the four of us got into a van and drove away. As soon as we left, the power of the Holy Spirit came upon us, and we started to laugh and laugh with the joy of the Lord. I was barely able to drive between the laughter bubbling up in me and the shrieks of joy coming from my friends in the van. We made it back to the Constellation Hotel and sat in the car laughing and wondering how we were going to make it into the lobby and to our rooms without making a commotion. I'm not talking about just a little laughter, but joy so full and expressive that we knew to most people, we must have looked intoxicated. It was suggested we try to think about something else other than the joy of the Lord. We got out of the van with no one daring to look at the other, for fear of another laughing fit. Things were going well until we walked through the door of the lobby. And then it all broke loose, and we scrambled to the elevator to hide from the impending rise of "living water" bubbling up within our souls.

Story Twenty-one: **God and Godiva Chocolates**

The next day wasn't any better as far as the laughing. We continued to have so much joy and looked forward to what God would do. We went to church, and after a morning meeting, we decided to go to the mall to do a little gift shopping. I was looking for something to take home to my wife. As we walked into the mall, we decided to split up. It seemed a little easier to maintain a state of composure from the laughter that continued to rise up on the inside as we fellowshipped together.

I came upon a Godiva chocolate shop and decided to look at the goodies. There was a young woman behind the counter who asked if I needed any help. I told her I was looking for a gift to take home to my wife. She asked where I was from, and I told her Washington state. **"Why are you in town?"** she asked. **"Haven't you heard what God is doing here in Toronto?"** I replied. **"No"** she said. I began to tell her of the outpouring of the Holy Spirit at the Airport Vineyard Church as well as the biblical account in Acts 2:4 upon the disciples.

I asked her if she went to church, and she said, **"Yes, I have just started going to a Catholic church, but I have a lot of questions, and I am not getting much out of the services."** I could tell that this young woman was very close to the kingdom of God and was hungry for more truth. I asked her if she had ever heard the terms "gospel" or "Good News" and if she knew what they meant. I began to explain to her the plan of salvation. Each time I would begin to share, a customer would come in, and I would have to stop and let her go to work. I was trying to be real sensitive to the fact that she was there to do a job and she needed the freedom to do that, yet I could sense the Holy Spirit opening up the opportunity to witness. I continued to explain, and she would ask more questions, but we continued to get interrupted. I knew the devil was trying hard to stop this conversation, so when the next customer came in and I stepped away from the counter, I began to pray, asking the Lord to send someone to intercede.

> And it shall come to pass, that before they call, I will answer; and while they are yet speaking, I will hear.
>
> Isaiah 65:24

What happened after that prayer was really exciting. When the customer left, I stepped back to the counter to continue sharing the gospel. A few minutes passed, and I noticed a lady standing to my left, so I turned and said, **"Do you need to talk to her?"** and she responded, **"No, I am listening to you."** Realizing that the Lord had sent me the intercessor I requested, I said, **"Would you please pray?"** and she replied, **"That is what I have been doing!"** I continued to share the gospel and answer the questions of the young lady selling chocolate. After a few minutes of ministering the Word to her and answering her questions, I said**, "Is there any reason why you couldn't receive Jesus Christ into your life right now?"** "No," she replied. So I said, **"Then would you like to do that right now?"** and she affirmed, **"Yes!"** So we prayed together, and when we finished, she literally glowed with the presence of the Lord!

Just as we were done praying, another employee came in the shop to take her place because her shift was over. (Good timing, Lord!) The three of us left the shop and gathered in the mall to talk more about what the Lord had done.

The lady whom the Lord sent told us that prior to coming into the chocolate shop, she was in a seminar listening to a lecture when she got this very strong impression to leave and go to the mall down the street. She finally gave in to the leading, not realizing that the Holy Spirit was the One doing the urging. When she got to the mall, she looked around and said to herself, **"What am I doing here?"** and then as she walked farther, she saw me talking to the chocolates lady. She was drawn to us, and that's when she overheard me preaching the gospel. She felt led to pray for the store to stay clear of shoppers and for the heart of the young woman to be open to the gospel. God is so good!

Story Twenty-two: **"Frozen Chosen" or Chosen to Be Frozen?**

I was back from Toronto and excited about what God was doing. Renewal was starting to break out in different places. I was contacted by a local pastor who thought it would be good for me to get together with three men from his church who had been going out on the streets and witnessing. I agreed to meet with them and share some key principles in personal evangelism and how to put together an effective street witnessing team. I went to my computer and printed out several of the different outlines I had used in teaching on evangelism and figured I was ready to give these guys some teaching on the basics of soul winning. Well, God had something else in mind.

> Then he answered and spake unto me, saying, "This is the word of the LORD unto Zerubbabel, saying, 'Not by might, nor by power, but by my spirit,' saith the LORD of hosts."
>
> Zechariah 4:6

We got together at the church office in what we called the "war room." It was essentially a prayer room for intercessors to come in each day and pray for the church and the nations. As we sat down, I began to go through my usual way of teaching on personal evangelism. The next thing that followed was not on my agenda for training. I started to get what I only can describe as crunches in my spirit or belly. The more I tried to talk, the worse it got. I was getting a little embarrassed because it was becoming noticeable to the others in the room. I tried to explain it was the Holy Spirit and, of course, that only brought more looks and questions. One of the guys offered me a cough drop, and another suggested I see a doctor. Finally, out of frustration, and realizing I couldn't go on talking, I said, **"Oh well, let's just pray."** Praying for them is what, unaware to me, God was really wanting me to do all along. We can sure get in the way when we try to do things by formula or tradition.

Paul says in Romans 1:11, "For I long to see you in order that I may impart some spiritual gift to you, that you may be established."

The Lord was looking to impart not just knowledge, but an anointing on these three guys. I had them line up and the pastor stand behind them just in case. When I put my hand on the top of the first man, he fell over backward and started to laugh and then to roll back and forth. (This must be what they call a holy roller.) He then came to a stop and started to speak out in an unknown tongue or language, and then he gave the interpretation. It was a beautiful exhortation from the Holy Spirit to go out into the highways and byways and preach the gospel and reach the lost.

The next guy I came to was just a little concerned, but surrendered to the anointing as the Holy Spirit touched him and he went down and started to laugh and laugh. The third guy sort of took a step back and said, "I'm not sure I want this." I went ahead and prayed for him also. I didn't notice anything happening with him, but that was okay; God was in charge, not me. I looked at the pastor, and He was smiling and jokingly saying, **"What have you done to my people."** I said, **"I didn't do it."**

I left the room for a minute, and when I came back in, the first guy whom I prayed for was standing up. I walked over to say something to him when I noticed that he was standing very still, but in a stance that looked sort of like someone ready to move forward, like being sent off. I said, **"Are you okay?"** and he replied, **"I can't move."** His lips were the only thing moving, but his body was totally still as if frozen. I said, **"Does it hurt?"** and he sort of chuckled and said, **"No."** I personally had never seen this kind of sign and wonder, but had heard it happening in other revivals where a speaker or a believer was temporarily in a state of motionlessness. The book *A Diary of Signs and Wonders*, a classic by Maria Woodworth Etter, tells of similar experiences.

I told him not to worry; he, of course, wasn't because of the peace of the Lord and the understanding that God was doing something holy. I looked at my watch and realized I had to leave to meet my wife, and so I told the pastor I had to go. He chuckled, and replied, **"You can't leave him like this."** I again told him I didn't do it and that God was in control. I got on the phone and called up my pastor and told him he should come up to the office because there was a man frozen in the war room. I left and picked up my wife, telling her what the Lord had done. Later, from home, I called the office and asked my pastor if the man was still frozen, and He said, "No." Apparently, after nearly an hour, he came out of the room and asked him what God was doing, to which the pastor replied, **"Revival."** The guy laughed and fell flat on his face and was stuck to the floor!

Why would God do something like this? I have no idea, except to say it is simply a sign and a wonder. We can read in Acts 15:12:

> Then all the multitude kept silent and listened to Barnabas and Paul declaring how many miracles and wonders God had worked through them among the Gentiles.

According to Strong's concordance, the word "wonder" in this text is translated from "teras" (ter-as). This is where we get the word "teratology," the science that deals with unexplainable phenomena. **Teras denotes extraordinary occurrences, unusual manifestations**. Teras is always in the plural, associated with semeion (signs). Signs and wonders work together to touch man's intellect, emotions, and will.

Signs and wonders have always accompanied the moving of the Holy Spirit and the preaching of the Word of God. We should expect the supernatural to be a part of our lives as we serve the Lord and do His will, even if at times it means receiving criticism from others in the body of Christ. Rarely does the opposition to the supernatural come from the lost. Usually, I find tradition and unbelief within the church to be the greatest hindrance to it. To be sure, the excesses I have seen cause genuine concern, and there needs to be proper oversight by the leadership. When God pours out His Spirit in power, we need to embrace what God is doing, be on guard to what the devil is doing, and bring correction to what the flesh is doing. It takes wisdom to not have the mistakes of past revivals repeated. People become focused on meetings alone instead of intimacy with God and personal discipleship. They don't read their Bibles or spend time in prayer, and then they get off on some strange revelation or make manifestations the main thing. Renewal comes to bring us back to our first love, the Lord Jesus Christ. Revival restores the church's compassion for the lost and brings in a harvest. Reformation or transformation of the community is a result.

One of the Scriptures the Lord gave concerning my attitude about unusual manifestations is found in Isaiah 28:21-22: "For the LORD will rise up as at Mount Perazim, He will be angry as in the Valley of Gibeon—That He may do His work, His awesome work (unusual task), and bring to pass His act, His unusual act (extraordinary work). Now therefore, do not be mockers, lest your bonds be made strong." It is wisdom to not judge quickly something we don't understand just because our minds are offended by it. We could be closing our hearts to the very thing that could set us free. Our bonds could be made stronger by mocking what truly is of the Lord. Sometimes I think it can be better to take a posture of wait and see and look for fruit. I'm not saying we shouldn't question. We should just not be so quick to make a judgment in the natural, but ask the Lord for discernment when what we are experiencing in the realm of our five senses does not clearly violate Scripture.

Story Twenty-three: **Not the Magic Kingdom, the Kingdom of God!**

The phone rang. "Hello, is this the Daley residence?" asked the person on the other end. "Yes," I replied as the person on the other end began to quickly explain a sales promotion for my family and me. A local photography studio called inviting us to take part in its special monthly free photo session with the hope of selling us a full set. I was wondering how I could graciously hang up when all of a sudden, the joy of the Lord began to rise up on the inside. Jesus said, "Out of your spirit shall rivers of living water flow." I began to laugh with joy. The person on the other end said, "You must really enjoy life." I said, "Yes, I do! Ha, Ha (laughing out loud). **That's because I am in the kingdom. Do you know what the kingdom is?**" "No," she said. **"Well,"** I replied, **"it's not the Magic Kingdom, like at Disneyland, but it's the kingdom of God and its righteousness, peace, and joy in the Holy Spirit."**

She said, "Well, I would be happy just to be rid of this headache." "You have a headache?" I responded. "Yes," she said. "Well then, put your hand on your head. Is it there?" I asked. "Yes," said the woman on the other end. **"In Jesus' name, headache, I command you to come out!"** I prayed. **"Is it still there?"** "NO!" the saleslady replied, surprised. **"Well, the same Jesus that healed you is also the same One Who died for your sins so you could receive forgiveness and eternal life. Isn't that Good News?"** "Yes!"

You know I almost missed an opportunity to see God change a life. I almost cut her short on the phone, but what an adventure it is to witness for Jesus. The Lord is looking for just a little boldness from us, and we get the joy of watching Him take the natural and make it supernatural!

Story Twenty-four: **"Pier" Pressure**

It was early morning, and I had driven down to a local park set along the banks of Lake Washington. It is a beautiful place and hardly occupied. Most people go to the larger park, and a lone fisherman sitting on the pier was the only person who occupied the one where I was. I went for my usual walk along the nature trails and read and prayed. After some time, I headed back toward my vehicle and opened the door and got into the driver's seat. I gazed out toward the man sitting on the pier quietly fishing, watching him for a little while. I wondered if he had caught anything, and then I thought of the story in John 21:4-6 about Jesus and the disciples.

> But when the day was now breaking, Jesus stood on the beach; yet the disciples did not know that it was Jesus. Jesus therefore said to them, "Children, you do not have any fish, do you?" They answered Him, "No." And He said to them, "Cast the net on the right-hand side of the boat, and you will find a catch." They cast therefore, and then they were not able to haul it in because of the great number of fish.

As I started to leave, I heard these words in my heart, **"Go tell him to cast over on the right side."** I chuckled at the thought and dismissed it and continued to drive out the gate and up the road. Again the thought came to me very strongly, **"Go tell him to cast over on the right side!"** I laughed and said out loud, **"And I suppose when he does, a big fish will come up and grab his bait."** I then heard the Holy Spirit say to me, **"You won't know if you leave."** *Mmmm*, I thought, so I pulled over to the side and turned my van around and headed back to the park. I wanted to see this!

I brought the van to a stop and got out and headed toward the beach. He was sitting on a folding chair about twenty-five yards out on a pier that looped around to the beach. I looked at him for a few minutes and, raising my hands to my mouth, cupping them so the sound would carry and yelled, **"Have you caught anything?"** and he looked up and shook his head side to side. I hollered, **"Cast your line over on the right side."** He looked up and hollered back **"What did you say?"** I yelled back, **"Cast your line over on the right side!"** He looked over to the right and looked up at me and then with a shrug started to reel in his line. Once he had his line in, he directed his pole toward the right side and cast out in that direction. We waited. And waited. And waited. Nothing was happening.

This is not good, I thought, thinking all of heaven was having a good laugh about now. "Okay, Lord, what do I do now?" **"Go talk to him,"** the Spirit replied. So I began to walk over to the dock that extended out toward him, thinking he probably thinks I'm some kind of nut coming out to get him. When I reached Him, he looked at me and said with a hint of sarcasm, **"Did you say to cast over on the right side or the wrong side?"**

I figured I better talk fast, so I replied, **"Have you not read in the Scripture where Jesus told Peter to cast his net on the right side? Do you know why it was the right side?"** and He said, **"No, why?" "Because that's the side that had all the fish,"** I replied, smiling at him. He said, **"What are you, a preacher?"** I laughed and said, **"Yes."** He began to gather up his fishing gear, either because it was time to go, or else he was trying to get away from me. I wasn't sure, but I continued to make conversation. I gave him a helping hand and picked up his bucket of gear, and we started to head toward the beach. I said, "What's your name?" and he replied, "Clarence." He was an elderly black man, probably in his seventies or older, and so after a little talk about fishing and the weather, I asked him if he had ever heard the Good News. He told me of his mother, who was a Christian woman, and of his experience years ago in Sunday school when, as a young boy, he went forward to receive Christ into his life. He shared of the dry years since that day. Many years had passed, and Clarence was not in fellowship with the Lord or with God's people. He told me it had been a long time since he felt like he did that day.

By the time he finished the story, we had reached his car, and setting down his fishing pole, he opened the trunk to put the gear in. Knowing the Lord wanted me to pray for him, I said, **"Clarence, how would you like to experience the touch of God on your life again? How would you like to know His love for you like that day as a young boy when you first met the Lord?"** He replied, **"I would like that."** And so I said, **"Let's pray and invite the Holy Spirit to come."**

I took his hands and prayed a simple prayer to God to restore and to confirm to Clarence His faithfulness and His love to him. As we prayed, the sweet presence of the Holy Spirit came, and Clarence kind of sighed, and we both just sort of stood there, waiting on God. I prayed again for him and afterward encouraged him to go to church. When I looked him in the eye, I felt such a powerful love in my heart for him. I said, **"Clarence, I love you and will be praying for you."** He thanked me and got into his vehicle. As he drove away, it really shocked me the love that was in my heart for this man whom I had just met. God is love, and the Holy Spirit pours His love into our hearts. We are able to love because He first loved us. The love of God is perhaps one of the best witnessing tools in sharing your faith, and yet it is not a tool, but God Himself being manifest through His people. When people experience the love of God, it's like a fountain of water in a desert land. Even the most dry or hardened heart softens. We need to speak the truth in love. The Holy Spirit was right. If I did not go back, I would have missed a big catch for Him.

Sometime later, I was walking with a friend of mine named Bill along another pier at Colon Park, located on Lake Washington in Renton. We were fellowshipping and prayerfully asking the Lord to give us a divine appointment. We happened upon a man fishing off of the boardwalk and started to make conversation with him, asking if he had caught anything. He replied, **"No, just some tugs upon the lures."** I asked him what he was using, and he began to talk about his lures and the way he had been fishing. Since he was an older gentleman, I then asked him if he came here often and if he was retired? He said no, that he had injured his back and chest on the job and could no longer work. He told us he was wearing a thick wrap like a brace around his chest to give support. He even invited me to feel it on his chest, which I did. He went on to tell us he had been to the doctor and had physical therapy, but that he wasn't any better and was depressed because He needed to go back to work but was unable because of the pain.

I then asked him if he would be open to another option. He said, **"Sure, what would that be?"** I asked him if we could pray for him and believe God for healing. I went on to say that God loved him and wanted him to be healed so he would be able to work again. He said something to the effect of, **"Well, it couldn't hurt."** I said, **"Well, it could really help,"** and so he started to reel in his line. Once he got it all reeled in, he grabbed his pole and looked to us for prayer. We led him over to a bench nearby, where we sat down. I took out my pocket New Testament, and I shared with him the Scripture in Mark 16:18, where Jesus said believers would lay hands on the sick, and they would recover. After sharing a few more Scriptures to build his faith up, we asked his permission to lay hands on him. He replied yes, and so Bill and I did and prayed a simple prayer binding and casting out a spirit of infirmity and commanding the pain to go and for healing of his muscles and nerves around his chest and back. I did not feel anything while praying, but he remarked how he felt heat. That caused his faith to rise, so we told him to stand up, and we asked on a scale between one and ten how he felt. The look on his face was priceless when he realized the pain was almost all gone. He kind of stuttered and said it's about an eight! I said, **"Good, let's believe for one hundred percent!"** We prayed again, and all the pain left! Then he got real emotional and started to cry, saying, **"I don't believe this is happening!"** We told him he could believe it! And then he actually said, **"Where you guys when I needed you almost a year ago?"** I laughed and said, **"Well, we are here now, but, more importantly, so is the Lord, and He wants to be a part of your life."** I asked him if he would like to give his heart to the One Who just healed him, and after sharing some important salvation Scriptures, Bill and I had the joy of leading him to the Lord. It was a great time as we hugged him and walked with him from the bench to the park's edge. He was so excited to be on his way home and tell his wife what had just happened. Glory to God! Remember when Jesus witnessed to the woman at the well in the fourth chapter of the Gospel of John and the disciples, having returned from buying food, urged Him to eat, and Jesus said, **"I have meat to eat of which you do not know"**? Well, I was told by a friend that John Wimber once said, **"The Meat is in the streets."** I think he had that right.

> For I long to see you, that I may impart unto you some spiritual gift, to the end ye may be established.
>
> Romans 1:11

Impartation

Paul tells us in Romans 1:11 of a principle that can change lives. He has in his heart the desire to visit these believers and impart, to share what God has given him. A key word in this text is the word "gift." It is the Greek word *khar-is-mah*, charisma. Charisma is "a gift of grace, a free gift, divine gratuity, spiritual endowment, miraculous faculty." It is especially used to designate the gifts of the Spirit, as in 1 Corinthians 12:4-10. Paul desired to impart "some" spiritual gift so that these believers may be established. According to Strong's Exhaustive Concordance, this word means "to be set, to be confirmed and to turn resolutely in a certain direction." According to Webster's dictionary, to be established is "to be set up, as in a business or government; to prove or to demonstrate; to establish one's cause or law, to bring about efforts."

Paul is saying here, "I have something you need. It is a grace gift. Freely I have received it, and freely I give it to you. I received it as a gift from God, and I want to impart, or share, it with you. You need this in order to be established in what the Lord has called you to do and to continue to go in that direction and further accomplish God's will." The following story, number twenty-six, brought this revelation into my life in a very powerful way.

Story Twenty-five: **The Streets of San Francisco,**
A Holy Ghost Production

The four of us—Mark, Steve, his son, and I—stepped off the train and onto the BART station in downtown San Francisco. We walked over and got onto the escalator that led us up to the street level of town. We had come from Oakland to do a little sightseeing. As we ascended up the escalator to the street surface, it became evident we were in a spiritually needy part of town. You didn't need a lot of discernment to see or feel the oppression in this particular city block; even the sidewalk billboards of abstract art and graphic pictures were oppressive. This place could surely use some salt and light. As we walked further away from the BART station, we noticed a large banner about half a block away with big letters: "JESUS, THE WAY!" We looked at one another, smiled, and headed toward the spiritual oasis. When we got closer, we saw a man wearing dark blue sunglasses speaking into a microphone connected to a loudspeaker, preaching his heart out. Scripture verse after Scripture verse came rolling off his lips to the seemingly deaf ears of those walking by.

As we approached, one of the Christian brothers came up and gave us a tract. Steve was wearing a T-shirt with the Seattle Revival Center logo SRC printed on it, and the brother passing out tracts noticed it and asked, "What is SRC, and what brings you here?" Steve told him about SRC and also about the renewal meetings we were having across the bay in Oakland at a Four Square Church. Then the guy jokingly said, **"What did you come over to the city for, to get oppressed? Christians don't come over here very often."** The way he put it was kind of funny, yet ironically true. At times it seemed the dark spiritual forces of this city were saying, "Go ahead, make my day." He then exclaimed, **"Hey, you guys got an anointing coming off you. Do you wanna preach?"** I turned to look at the guy with the microphone and thought to myself, *What is he doing with those dark blue glasses on?* (When I speak to people, I like them to see my eyes, and vice versa, the eyes being the window to the soul.) Steve said, **"Go ahead, Greg, this is your specialty."** I love to preach on the street, but as I watched and heard this man, I just couldn't get a vision to do what he was doing. Sure he was quoting Scripture like a machine gun, but where was the anointing? I asked our street brother who we first met if they had seen many get saved, and he paused and said someone got saved last week. I asked him if anyone got healed, and he said, "No." Then he asked, **"Have you seen anyone get healed?"** We replied that in the meetings we had been in, it was not uncommon to see the Lord confirm His Word with signs and wonders. He was excited about the reports we gave him.

As this man preached, I watched the people walk by and appear to be seemingly oblivious to what was being said. Pretty soon the brother standing by us said, **"His time is about up. Which one of you is going to be first?"** Steve and I looked at each other, and he said, **"Go ahead, Greg."** I looked at the guy with the blue shades holding the microphone in our direction and with great boldness pushed Steve toward the microphone, saying, **"You first."**

When he took the microphone and began talking, it was really fresh, kind of like coming to hear a familiar neighbor give an encouraging talk. Steve began to introduce himself to the people of San Francisco, and immediately the anointing became very apparent. It was as if the atmosphere on that corner suddenly changed. I don't know if Steve felt it or noticed, but all of a sudden, people began to turn their heads in his direction. *Now this is more like it!* I thought. Steve began to address the people about the love of God and talk to them with such warmth and humor. He probably only used a few Scriptures, but the picture he was telling of Jesus was coming in clear.

Steve motioned to me, and I made my way over to the

loudspeaker. He passed the microphone to me, and I began to tell the people that we were here to tell them that Christianity was not a religion, but a relationship with a loving Father Who demonstrated His love for us by sending His Son. I began to tell them of all Jesus did for them at the cross and that He did it out of love. He not only bore our sins, but He carried away our sicknesses and diseases. I shouted over the microphone, **"If you are listening to these words and you are sick and would like prayer, please come up, and we will pray for you."** I passed the microphone to the next street preacher who was stepping up to minister, and as I did, a lady came up and said she was a Christian and wanted prayer for healing. We prayed for her healing, and then a young man who had been watching walked over and said, **"You know, I have been standing here for some time, and God began to talk to me about going on the street and preaching, but I couldn't see how I could do what I have been seeing that other guy do. Then you two walked up and started talking, and I said to myself, "I could do that!"** He then looked at us and remarked, **"You guys seem kind of healthy or something."** We both laughed because renewal was kind of like being in a health club. His comment reminded me of a billboard I had seen on the freeway driving near Daily City. It was a picture of gentle rain falling, and over it were the words, in bold print, "Refresh, Renew, Restore, Results," with the name of a local health club under it. This statement concerning the natural was very prophetic concerning what God was doing spiritually in His church. We encouraged him to step out and let God use him on the streets, and then he asked for prayer. As we prayed for him, the joy of the Lord rose up in his spirit, and he began to get real happy and excited about what God was doing on the inside. When we finished praying, I turned, and the brother who was wearing the dark blue sunglasses was standing next to me. He took off his glasses and said, **"I don't know why I am wearing these."** (My thoughts exactly.) When I looked into his eyes, I could see how dry this dear brother's soul was. He then said, **"You know, I feel like such a novice."** I was amazed at his statement because here was a Christian who could quote just about every Bible verse you could think of concerning salvation, heaven, or hell, yet in his heart, he felt truly inadequate.

We began to encourage him in the Lord and in the work he was doing, reminding him of the need to stay anointed with the Holy Spirit because he was on the front lines of the battle against Satan and every mind-blinding spirit that was trying to keep the gospel hidden from the people. The words we preach need to be ablaze with the fire and anointing of the Spirit of God. It is not by our power nor by our might, but by His Spirit. Then he asked for prayer, so we began to pray, calling on the Spirit of God to anoint anew this warrior for Christ. Laying hands on him was like laying hands on a dry, hard sponge, but soon he began to soften as he soaked in the living water. It was wonderful to see the change in his countenance and soul.

We left the group of street preachers and headed back toward the BART station. As we approached the escalator to descend down to catch the train, we saw another street preacher. This time it was a small Asian man standing on a container for height and preaching to a crowd of people who were in line to catch the cable car. I must say he picked a good spot, for he had a captive audience because if they wanted to stay and wait for the trolley, they had to listen to him. The four of us watched the faces of those standing in line, and again it seemed that his words were falling on deaf ears. We began to pray for him, asking the Holy Spirit to anoint his words and to open up the hearts of the people. All of a sudden, he began to laugh. The outburst of laughter startled him, and it also caused everyone to turn and look up at him. He then remarked, **"Well, I guess I have a sense of humor after all,"** continuing to laugh. He also now had the people's attention and continued to minister. Sometimes

God uses the foolish things to confound the wise, even those who seem wise in their own eyes.

Because it was time to catch our train, we couldn't stay, so we headed down the escalator and to the train. It occurred to me that God was showing us something about the anointing through these two incidents, as well as the way we as Christians may need to change our approach to preaching the gospel. I think sometimes we discredit the cause of Christ by our methods of evangelism. Many times instead of asking the Father what He wants to do, we look to methods or patterns of things we have seen others do. Some of the hellfire and brimstone preaching I have seen does more to discredit the gospel than bring the lost in. Another thing the Holy Spirit was showing us had to do with impartation, and the other with proximity, or the nearness of the anointing from other believers. Later on that evening, when we were holding services in a church in Oakland, I felt led to share with the people what happened to us on the streets of San Francisco. I told the story of the street preacher who spoke the Word but seemed spiritually dry. At the end of the sermon, I gave an altar call for anyone who felt they were called in the area of evangelism. Half a dozen people or so came forward for prayer. I stood before a middle-aged man, who said to me, **"I am a street preacher who ministers in San Francisco, and I am dry and need what you have."** I took him by the hand and led him over to an area that was clear of people. I waited on the Lord for a moment and then prayed, **"Father, if I am an evangelist, give this man all the anointing you have given me for evangelism, and more."** As I placed my hand on his head, the power of God hit us both at the same time, and we both started laughing at the exact same second, and then stopped in amazement at the exact second, and then took off on cue speaking the same words of awe and exclamation as if we were in sync or stereo. Even our expression and the redness of our faces, I was told later, were the same. I turned in amazement to a friend next to me, and she had this surprised look on her face as she exclaimed, **"What is this?"** I heard the Holy Spirit say to me, **"Impartation,"** and with that, the man I was praying for fell backward and landed on the floor, shaking under the power of God.

I have never seen this particular sign or wonder of impartation before, nor since. I have always believed in the laying on of hands for gifts to be imparted, but this particular evening brought a fresh understanding of it to me. I believe God was showing what was taking place in the spirit by manifesting it in the natural. This man and the rest of the people who had come forward to receive an impartation from the Holy Spirit were not disappointed. I believe this is part of equipping the saints for the work of the ministry. I think it is wrong for men and women who are called to ministry to selfishly hold on to the gifts and take a one-man-show attitude. We have been given gifts to impart to others. After all, the gifts of the Holy Spirit are just that: gifts. Freely we have received, so freely we need to give.

We have the apostle Paul's example in Romans 1:11 and also an example in the Old Testament with Moses.

> Then I will come down and speak with you there, and I will take of the Spirit who is upon you, and will put Him upon them; and they shall bear the burden of the people with you, so that you shall not bear it all alone. And the LORD said to Moses, "Is the LORD'S power limited? Now you shall see whether My word will come true for you or not." So Moses went out and told the people the words of the LORD. Also, he gathered seventy men of the elders of the people, and stationed them around the tent. Then the LORD came down in the cloud and spoke to him; and He took of the Spirit who was upon him and placed Him

upon the seventy elders. And it came about that when the Spirit rested upon them, they prophesied. But they did not do it again.

Numbers 11:17, 23-25

I would like to add that many Bibles, such as the New Spirit Filled Life Bible, have in their margins an alternate translation of "**and they did not cease.**" Taken from the Vulgate—an ancient translation of the Bible into Latin, translated and edited by Jerome, or St. Jerome, who was commissioned by Pope Damascus to translate the original Greek and Hebrew texts into Latin.

Proximity or Nearness

If you are born again and filled with the Holy Spirit, you are a vessel of the anointing of God. The more we understand this, the more we will be aware of how the Holy Spirit can touch the lives of people around us. For example, we read in Acts 5:14-16: "And all the more believers in the Lord, multitudes of men and women, were constantly added to their number; to such an extent that they even carried the sick out into the streets, and laid them on cots and pallets, so that when Peter came by, at least his shadow might fall on any one of them. And also the people from the cities in the vicinity of Jerusalem were coming together, bringing people who were sick or afflicted with unclean spirits; and they were all being healed.

Here we have God adding to the church; they are increasing in number (verse 14), and people begin to carry the sick out into the streets (note: not into the church building). Why? Because something was happening out in the streets when people who were sick came into contact with a believer. Peter walked by some of these sick folk, his shadow touched them, and they were healed. Was it Peter's shadow that healed the people? No, of course not. It was the anointing of God in and on Peter that brought life and healing to where there was sickness. One evening in a service, I was preaching on Malachi 4:2: "But for you who fear My name the sun of righteousness will rise with healing in its wings; and you will go forth and skip about like calves from the stall."

The sun of righteousness here refers to the glory. Note the word "sun," and not "son." The sun is a blaze of fire and light. It speaks of the glory of God arising with healing in its wings, and the church folk (those who fear, reverence the name of the Lord) were going forth, bringing that glory to the sick for healing. We should not look for the glory to come down out of the sky, but to rise up and out of the body of Christ.

I was describing how the anointing of God for healing was coming on the body of Christ in a greater measure, and we would see those who fear His name begin to rise with healing, and we would see and experience what the early Christians saw on the streets, and how at times, just by being near the anointing of God in believers, you can be healed.

We gathered after the message for a time of worship, and I felt led to invite all the people to the front to gather and worship together. As we were singing unto the Lord, a lady from the second row made her way to the front, and as she got within several feet of where I was, she began to stumble backward and finally landed in a chair. I took note, seeing she was not hurt, and then continued to focus on the presence of the Lord. After a time of worship, I went over to the lady to find out what had happened to her. She began to exclaim very excitedly that she had been healed. She went on to relate that as soon as she got up to the front near me, the power of God hit her and she was healed of a severe back injury. We rejoiced together, and I had her get up and share with the people what Jesus had done. The Lord began to remind me of the message on Malachi 4 and Acts 5 that I had spoken on that evening. God was confirming His Word.

What took place that night had to do with the anointing on the body of Christ, the glory of His presence upon His people. No one prayed for this lady; she just took a step of faith and walked into the glory and was healed.

The woman with the issue of blood in the fifth chapter of Mark got closer and closer to Jesus until she touched Him and power went out of Him and she was made well. She took a step of faith and touched Him, and Jesus said, "Your faith has made you well." Some will remark and say, "Jesus had the Spirit without measure." This is true, yet Jesus on earth was also our example of what it meant to be a Son walking in the Father's love and doing the works of His Father.

> For He whom God has sent speaks the words of God; for He gives the Spirit without measure. The Father loves the Son, and has given all things into His hand.
>
> John 3:34-35

Jesus received **the Spirit** in fullness, with nothing held back, and He alone has universal authority. **However**, since this endowment of the Holy Spirit is given to **He whom God has sent,** John 20:21 would suggest a similar unlimited resource of Holy Spirit fullness is available to obedient disciples of His (Jesus'): "So Jesus said to them again, "Peace to you! As the Father has sent Me, I also send you." Do we fully realize the potential of God that dwells in us by His Holy Spirit? One day I was reading in the eighth chapter of Matthew's Gospel the story of the centurion pleading with Jesus, saying, "Lord my servant is lying at home paralyzed, dreadfully tormented." Jesus said to him, "I will come and heal him." As soon as I finished reading the Lord's reply, the Holy Spirit said to me in what seemed almost an audible voice, **"When are you going to start doing that?"** I was really taken aback and, to be honest, almost offended by the

Lord's directness. I heard someone say once, When God asks you a question, it is not because He doesn't know the answer. Being a pastor at the time He spoke this, I have had many opportunities to pray for the sick—most of the time in church services when the call is given to pray for the sick in accordance to James 5:14 or during a visit to someone's home. After a brief moment of my complaining to the Lord about what I thought was an unfair question since He is the One Who heals the sick and not me, He began to explain to me He really wanted to challenge my thinking as well as the body of Christ in praying only for the sick when they come to church or a special service. The Lord was emphasizing His words, "**I will come** and heal him." He was speaking about going to where the sick are. Not just those who are sick physically, but emotionally as well. They are outside the church walls in our neighborhoods and in the marketplace. Why wait for them to come in to a service to pray for them. I am not suggesting we just run outside with a bottle of oil and smear anyone who looks sick like "drive-by healings." I'm talking about having the Father's heart of compassion and moving in that compassion, no matter what the setting, especially outside the four walls of our local church. Sure we need to be led by the Holy Spirit, but sometimes don't we use that as a religious excuse not to pray or expect God to use us when He many times is ready to confirm His Word as we step out in faith? To quote John Wimber, sometimes faith is truly spelled R I S K.

My wife and I were in a local store shopping during the Christmas season. We spotted a cabinet that we thought might work in our entryway and walked over to take a look. There was another women standing in front of it with a tape measure, getting measurements. She dropped her tape and then looked at me rather embarrassed and said, **"Would you please help me and pick up my tape? I had a stroke a while back, and sometimes when I bend over, I lose my balance."** When I heard her say she had suffered a stroke,

I felt compassion for her. I smiled, said I would be glad to help, picked it up, and handed it to her. She thanked me, and I turned to walk away. As I moved away from her, the desire to do something about it remained. As I approached my wife, I said to Mary, **"I believe I'm supposed to pray for this woman."** I turned and walked several steps back to her and simply relayed to her what I had spoken to my wife. I told her I believed Jesus wanted to heal her and asked her if she would like to receive prayer. She replied, **"Yes, I would like that."** And so I prayed for her healing. Then I asked her to try and do something she normally couldn't do to see what God had done. She replied, **"I would like to try bending over, but is it okay if I wait until I get home just in case I fall?"** I said, **"No way, lady, you bend over right this minute!** (Just kidding!) I, of course, assured her that would be just fine and told her to give it a try when she got home. She thanked me, and I left.

I do not know if she went home and tried or to what extent God healed her, but I do know I acted on the compassion that was in my heart at that moment. We may not always see the results right away, but we must be obedient and leave the results up to God. Jesus said in Mark 16 believers shall lay hands on the sick, and they shall recover. The word "recover" means to begin to amend, or get better from that time forward. It may happen immediately or take time, but let's believe and trust God that from the moment we pray, He is at work bringing to pass His perfect will.

Jesus said to the nobleman whose son was sick at Capernaum, "Unless you people see signs and wonders, you will by no means believe" (John 4:48). Jesus did not regard signs and wonders as an end in themselves. Rather, they were at the very least intended to bring the recipients of the miracle to faith in Christ.

Signs and wonders can be a calling card to the gospel. We should be **expecting** and **believing** God to do the miraculous like He did through the disciples in the book of Acts. Jesus is the same yesterday, today, and forever.

The Lord drove this point home (literally) one day when a magazine was delivered to our house by mistake. It was a home and office organizational magazine, wrapped in clear plastic. The number of the house it was postmarked to was the same as ours, but the street was different, and the last name on the label was similar to our last name but spelled differently. So we brought it into the house with the rest of the mail and put it on the kitchen table to go out the next day. The following morning, my son-in-law was talking to me about the importance of believing God for miracles. He was sharing some thoughts and quotations he had recently read. God had been challenging him recently to expect and believe for the miraculous. He looked down and read the printed slogan on the edge of the magazine. It said, **"There are no miracles for those that have no faith in them."** He read this out loud to my wife and me. Then he turned the magazine around and read out loud its cover name, **"Real Simple."** My wife, Mary, said, **"Do you think God is trying to say something here?"** Well, we all felt this was one of those God moments. He sure knows how to get our attention when He wants to.

As my wife and I left for work, I grabbed the magazine and put it in the mailbox for the afternoon pickup and thought about the incident as we drove away. It was amazing to me how the Holy Spirit used a secular magazine, delivered to our house by accident, to challenge us with a truth of the kingdom that morning. All things are possible to them that believe.

Story Twenty-six: **Fishing With the Net**

I can remember when the home PC and the Internet first began appearing in the marketplace for consumers to purchase. Some Christians actually began referring to them as the "beast" referred to in Revelations. Well, it may be a tool used by the devil, but it also can be a tool used by the church for the kingdom of God. I have an evangelist friend named Jerry, who was telling me of some people he had led to the Lord by going into the chatrooms and witnessing. This really excited me, so I decided to give it a try. There are Christian chatrooms that can be edifying, and most will pray for you if you desire. The secular ones are quite different and not unlike the atmosphere of a tavern or bar or even worse. Most of the people who use these rooms have screen names such as CybeSims1 or Teedoff or MorbidBob, to name just a few that are not real offensive. I do not suggest that any Christian go into these rooms unless he has a goal and a purpose that is godly. My goal is to witness, and my purpose is to destroy the works of the devil.

I decided to come up with a screen name of my own apart from my real name that I use for personal email response. So I came up with the screen name **BAWSAR**. I liked the sound of it! It is a Hebrew word translated **"good tidings"** in Psalm 96:2: "Sing to the LORD, bless His name; proclaim good tidings (bawsar) of His salvation from day to day."

The work was used to describe a messenger who, by the expression on his face, told of good news. By extension, every messenger from a battlefield carrying news became known as bawsar.

I decided I would try going online late in the evening, so I waited until midnight. Armed with a code name and the armor of God, I leaped into cyberspace and headed for the chatroom known as the Best Lil Chathouse number 3. The room was filled with a dozen or more people. Some where talking; others where waiting and watching their screens.

The following is how it appeared on my monitor.

Greetings everyone! (I typed in)

Hey Baw, how's it going! (someone typed back)

Does anyone need prayer? (I typed in; no answer, as I waited for a reply)

Is there anyone who needs prayer for physical healing or any other need? (I again tried)

I don't believe in God. (typed back someone with a screen name I can't repeat)

Why not? (I typed)

I have my own beliefs, don't force your God on me. (came the reply)

Tell me about your God. (I said)

That's personal. (he replied)

What has your God done for you lately? Has he forgiven you, has He healed you when you were sick? (I said)

Your God is a product of your mind. (he replied)

No, my God is real, He died on a cross for my sins and He rose from the dead and He is alive forever more, His name is Jesus! (I replied)

I typed in John 3:16 and sent it on to the chatroom. This caused a flurry of replies. At this point, others began to come to his defense, and some became quite angry. The devil did not like a Christian coming into his territory to witness. The language is supposed to be monitored on these chatrooms, and everyone is supposed to not use foul language, but that is not at all the case. Rules are broken constantly, and people say what they want to. Some have even gotten pretty good at typing in pictures that are meant to offend. I stepped out of the chatroom and began to look into other chatrooms. I hadn't been out for more than two minutes when I got a private email sent to me from the guy who had been offensive toward my witnessing. He wanted to talk privately, so we went into a private room, and then he began to tell me how he used to be a Christian but stopped going to church and reading his Bible. He was simply a young man who lived at home and was just hurting and in need of a friend. We spent some time talking, and I encouraged him to get back into the Word and church. He thanked me for taking the time to talk to him, and because it was now after 1 A.M., he was tired and needed to go to bed. So many people will put on a front about God or respond in anger or be defensive because on the inside they are just people who have been hurt or deceived. But if we stick with them and don't fall into the trap of letting the devil use them to shock or offend us by their comments, many times they will open up and get real.

One time I was witnessing in another room when a woman came into the chatroom and greeted everyone. I responded with a "Hello" and asked her how she was doing. She was aware of what was going on because all the conversations are displayed on the screen, and you can scroll to the most recent talk.

Not too good Bawsar. (was her reply)
I just had cyber sex with my boyfriend and I'm feeling bad about it. (was her reply)

Cybersex? I thought. It is amazing what people do with technology. This was a new one for me. I thought I had heard just about everything. I continued the conversation by telling her about the love of God and the willingness of the Lord to forgive our sins and to cleanse us from it. I told her forgiveness was there for her, and she just needed to repent and receive it. She thanked me and said she was worried about her boyfriend coming over because she didn't know if she could have the strength to do what was right. I told her that the Bible says to be strong in the Lord and that she was right, she wouldn't have the strength in herself, but that Jesus could help her to do what was right. I spent some time talking to her and encouraging her to look to the Lord. She eventually said it was late and she had to go and then thanked me for what she referred to as kind words. I signed off and spent some time praying for her and the others I had witnessed to.

AOL has a place for you to give a short description of who you are. Many choose not to use it, but I decided it would be a good way to make conversations center on the Lord. One evening, I was searching out a chatroom and came across a person all alone. No one else was signed into the room. He or she was just kind of sitting there. I signed in and said:

Hello!
(no reply)
How are you tonight? (I replied; still no answer)

Her screen name was somewhat provocative, so I decided to comment on it since that's the reason most people use them, that is, to get a reaction.

That's an interesting screen name you got there. (I typed)
BE PATENT I DUNT KNOW WHAT IM DOiNG (was her reply, complete with misspellings. When people want to talk loud or make a point, they always type in capitals.)
Sure, that's ok. I'll wait, take your time. (I wrote)
This is my first time. (she wrote)
That's ok, you're doing good. I typed)
You seem like a peaceful person. (she wrote)
Yes, that's because I know the Prince of peace—JESUS. (I said)
What are you, a Christian or a preacher? (she wrote)
Both, actually. (I said, knowing she probably checked my online bio. I decided to look up her bio to see if she had more information about herself. Her bio said she was from

my state and that she liked nude recreation.)

That's an unusual form of outdoor activity. (I typed)

Why, what does it say? (she wrote)

It says you like nude recreation. (I typed)

Oh no, is that really on there! (her spelling was starting to improve by now)

Yes, it is. (I replied)

I am really sorry. (she wrote)

I've seen worse. (which is really true, when you witness like this)

Where do you go to church? (she said)

Word of His Grace in Kirkland. (I typed)

Do you know the Lord? (I asked)

No. (she replied; I waited, and she again typed in)

I used to know Him. (she wrote)

What happened? (I wrote)

From then on, she began to tell me about her life and family. She spoke about how she lost her son in an accident and how she had become angry with God. She was now bitter and not serving the Lord. I told her that I could not imagine what it would be like to lose a child and that it must have been hard. I began to minister to her about the grace of God and how when bad things happen, it isn't wise to say it's God's fault. We don't always understand these things. Jesus said the devil comes to steal, kill, and destroy, but He came that we might have life and have it more abundantly. The Bible tells us every good and perfect gift comes down from the Father of lights. God was not the One to blame. He wants to heal your hurts. He demonstrated His love for us by giving up His own Son. I asked her if I could pray for her and lead her back to the Lord. To my excitement and joy, she said yes! She also wanted to tell me more about herself and where she had come from. So I listened and prayed as she spoke of these things.

When she was done, I told her that I would pray, but

because I had to type in the prayer, she needed to be patient and give me time to write, and when I was done, I would type the word "amen." You can only type in so much on a line, and then you have to send what you have typed. She said she would wait and then she told me what her real name was so I could properly address her. As I began to type out a prayer, I felt led to speak or type in words that brought deliverance. It was truly amazing how the Holy Spirit took those typed words and anointed them to bring deliverance and healing to this one who was out of fellowship with the Father. The Bible says in Psalms 107:20, "He sent His word and healed them, and delivered them from their destructions." As I wrote earlier, the Internet can be a tool for evil or for good—a tool used by the devil to promote his agenda and influence man, or by men and woman yielded to the Spirit of God to bring light where there is darkness. Just think, you can go to another city or state or even foreign country and go right into the homes of these people who don't know the Lord and bring the Good News. This is taking the land. This is the Great Commission.

Story Twenty-seven: **Elmo's Fire**

I was driving by a park one day to find a place to walk around and pray when I noticed a bunch of youth gathered around talking. Some were smoking, and they just seemed to be hanging out. I said to myself, "What a great opportunity for someone or a group from a local church to minister to these youth who hang out here." Right after that thought, I heard the Holy Spirit say, **"What about you—what are you going to do about it?"** (Don't you just love it when the Lord brings it home and to the point?) I thought about that, said, "okay," reached over to get a couple of gospel tracts, left the car, and headed for the group of teens.

As I started to get near, I began to pray in the spirit quietly and waited on the Lord. I felt the leading to just walk by them, and so I did notice the several that were smoking and others that appeared to be putting away other items into their pockets. Perhaps they thought I was a policeman. I kept walking and stopped about fifty yards beyond them and then began to spend some time praying for them and asking God to show me what to do. I had a picture in my spirit of God doing something good, so I proceeded back to their midst. I walked up and greeted them with a simple **"Hello, how are you guys doing?"** There were about half a dozen of them and one girl.

They looked at me rather suspiciously, and one of them responded with a nod and a few words. I could sense they were curious about my appearance, and so I just told them I was in town on some business and was passing by the park and thought it was great for this small city to have a park located in the middle of it. I asked them if they came here often, and they replied that there wasn't much of anything else to do. I mentioned that I had noticed that for a town of about 5,000, they had quite a few churches, and one of the kids remarked that there were about thirty-five churches. I said, **"That's a lot of churches for a town this size,"** and they agreed.

Kneeling down on one knee to be closer, I asked them if they thought God was in all those churches. One of the youths replied, **"Well, God is everywhere,"** to which I said, **"Yes, God is omnipresent—that is to say He sees everything, and His Spirit can be everywhere, but how do you know He is in every single church?"** The same kid replied, **"I don't know."** So I said, **"Well, if I were to visit your house and were to walk into your living room and turn on a lamp, I would see some light in the house. And if I were to take the light bulb out and put my finger in the socket and turn the switch on, I would know that you had power in that lamp. In the same way, it seems to me if God is present in a church, there ought to be not just good sermons, but some signs of His power and activity because the apostle Paul said that the kingdom of God is not in word, but in power."**

> For the kingdom of God does not consist in words, but in power.
>
> 1 Corinthians 4:20

One of the youths sitting across from me, who was smoking his cigarette, spoke up and said, **"Well, I believe unless you're living on the edge, you are just taking up space."** I said, **"Wow, that's really good; that's radical thinking. That sounds like something Jesus would say. What's your name?"** and he replied, "Elmo." I said, **"Hey, Elmo, how would you like to experience the power of God?"** and he kind of looked at his buddies and laughed and said, **"Nah! I don't think so."** I looked at him and said, **"Now, Elmo, you said unless you are living on the edge, you are just taking up space."** And so knowing that I had him by his own words, he said, **"Okay,"** and we both stood up.

Then I said to all of them, **"We are now going to have church. The church is not a building because God doesn't dwell in buildings made by men's hands, but rather the church is a people, the body of Christ. So here we are in this park gathered together, and we are going to have church. Now in many churches, the preacher would give a message and pray for an individual who came forward."** So I said, **"Elmo, you come over here, and now we also need to have an usher or a catcher, someone to stand behind the one we are praying for. That can be you,"** I said as I pointed to the tallest youth. I said, "You stand behind Elmo, but don't touch him. Just be ready to catch him if he falls." So this guy stood about ten feet behind Elmo, and I said, "No, that's too far; you need to get closer." Then I looked at Elmo and said, "You stand here, and you probably should put your cigarette down so you don't get burned, and why don't you take your hat off because I'm going to put my hand on your head." I asked him if that would be okay, and he agreed. By this time, the rest of the youth were standing there looking at the three of us lined up, and they were wondering what was going to happen next. I said to Elmo, **"I'm going to ask for the Holy Spirit to just come and touch you with His presence. Are you ready?"** and he nodded.

I simply placed my I hand on his head and said, **"Come, Holy Spirit!"** The Holy Spirit came upon Elmo and me as we stood in that park. I could feel the power of God flowing through me, and then Elmo went flying backward, along with the catcher behind him, and they both landed on the ground. Elmo got up and had this startled look on his face from just experiencing something he had never encountered before. I said, **"Elmo, did you feel that?"** And with an excited voice, he said, **"Yeah!"** I said, **"What did it feel like?"** and he replied, **"Heat! It felt like heat."** I said, **"What else did it feel like?"** and he replied with a lot of emotion, **"It was like being on acid."** Now I know that is probably not a very sacred or holy way to describe the touch of the Holy Spirit, but you have to remember, this kid didn't go to church, and he wasn't saved, and he had never in his life had a supernatural encounter with the Holy Spirit. So I just laughed as he began to explain to his buddies what it felt like.

About this time, the rest of the youth were keeping their distance, and several started to doubt and make fun of Elmo. The amazing thing was Elmo started to witness to his buddies of the power of God by saying, **"Hey, listen, he placed his hand of me, and something hit me, you guys."** So I turned to Elmo and said, **"Elmo, now that you just had an experience with power, you need to know the One who gives the power. His name is Jesus."** I went on to tell him he now had a serious choice to make because he had experienced something many do not, and so he was going to be held accountable for it. I began to share the Good News with him, and I asked him if he would like to give his life over to Jesus. He said, **"Right now?"** and I said, **"Yes, Elmo, right now! Forget about your friends for now. This is between you and God."** I went on to explain God's plan of salvation, and right there before all of his friends, this young man gave his heart to the Lord. Glory!

The exciting thing about this was that no one could tell this young man God hadn't touched him. Not even the peer pressure from his buddies caused him to turn away. Elmo quickly became the witness testifying to his friends of a supernatural God, but isn't that what Christianity is—a relationship with a living supernatural God Who raised the dead, walked on water, and created the heavens and the earth by the word of His power?

You know, we get excited about seeing the glory of God manifested in church services, looking for smoke and fire and gold and oil, and yes, that is glorious! But do you know what I believe God gets excited about? Souls coming to Christ and seeing Christ in you! The hope of glory. God desires to arise on the inside of you and in all His people to demonstrate His glory and power.

Arise, shine; for thy light is come, and the glory of the LORD is risen upon thee. For, behold, the darkness shall cover the earth, and gross darkness the people: but the LORD shall arise upon thee, and his glory shall be seen upon thee. And the Gentiles shall come to thy light, and kings to the brightness of thy rising.

Isaiah 60:1-3

God says, "Arise, shine, for your light has come." He didn't say *the* light has come. Many Christians think the glory of the Lord is going to come down out of heaven apart from you and cover the whole earth. No, God always has His vessels to fill and to dwell in. The Holy Spirit has been given, and His glory on the inside of you and me is going to arise and shine. And the Gentiles, according to verse 3, shall come to your light, and you are going to tell them of THE LIGHT, Jesus the Christ!

Didn't Jesus say that *you* are the light of the world? Matthew 5:14: "Ye are the light of the world. A city that is set on a hill cannot be hid." And in Matthew 5:16, He said, "Let your light so shine before men, that they may see your good works, and glorify your Father which is in heaven."

Let the church arise and shine. Let the church rise up and declare His wonders throughout the whole earth! We are living in exciting times, as God begins to pour out His Spirit upon all flesh, and those vessels of flesh begin to go into the entire world and declare His kingdom and His power and His glory!

Story Twenty-eight: **Painting Stories**

I was standing on the platform at Seattle Revival Center (SRC) during the ministry time when the guest speaker turned to me and prophesied, "God is sending you back into the marketplace and unto the nations." I fell over backward under the Spirit's power and lay there, bathing in the presence of the Holy Spirit. After I got up, I pondered the message. What did He mean "back into the marketplace"? I had been to other nations preaching. Was this word about distant lands or people groups around me? I was presently in full-time ministry, traveling and ministering renewal in churches as the Lord led. To be honest, I did not have any desire to leave full-time ministry and go back to working in the marketplace. This way of thinking is much of the problem with many in our churches today. We think the business or the marketplace is secular, and the church is sacred. God wants to move in both.

I soon began to learn that what God wants, God gets. Doors to preach began to close, and finances to travel and minister began to dry up. It kind of reminded me of the brook of Cherith in 1 Kings 17:3. In this story, the brook dried up, and the Lord sent the prophet Elijah to Zarephath in Sidon. Interestingly, Zarephath means refinement or place of refining. God was going to do some refining in me. Also, it was at Zarephath that provision came for the prophet, as well as a demonstration of God's power. It was here where Elijah raised the widow's son from the dead. I set the word aside in my heart and continued to serve the Lord.

Later on, the Lord brought another prophetic word to me that He was putting a new tool into my hands, and I would have the finances to do the things that were in my heart to do. The things that were in my heart to do at that time were to buy a home for my wife and family instead of renting and also to equip believers in the area of evangelism. Shortly after receiving the word about a new tool, the Holy Spirit led me to seek employment with a local painting company. I was hired and found myself back in the marketplace.

I found the painting industry to be quite a mission field. It seems a majority of the men I worked with were either ex-cons, drug and alcohol abusers, or generally just your average sinner in need of Jesus. I was assigned to a major remodeling project, working at a large apartment community that would take about a year to complete.

The first couple of weeks, I just settled in, learning what to do and what was expected. I believe as Christians, we need to set an example by working hard. The opportunities to witness will arise soon enough as those you work with see your faith in action through good work ethics and how you respond to life's situations. In 1 Peter 3:15, the Word says, "But sanctify the Lord God in your hearts, and always be ready to give a defense to everyone **who asks** you a reason for the hope that is in you, with meekness and fear." **Why do they ask you?** What would make a non-believer ask you about why you are a Christian? Could it be they see the way you work? Are you always on time? Do you put in an honest day's work? Do you use foul language or gossip? Is it how you respond to life's circumstances with grace, how you show mercy and do not talk as negatively as the others? I think it was St Augustine who said, "Witness, and if you must, use words." The apostle Paul writes, **"You are our epistle written in our hearts, known and read by all men; clearly you are an epistle of Christ"** (2 Corinthians 3:2-3a). Non-Christians are watching us, and many times, our actions and how we live are the biggest witnesses of what we believe.

Prior to being hired at the painting company, I had a meeting scheduled to minister on New Year's Eve in Bandon, Oregon, at a local church. God gave me favor, and the boss gave me an extra day off to travel. The day before leaving, one of the guys I worked with asked me what I would be doing in Bandon. I told him of the ministry, and he gave me a new nickname, "Preach." Soon everyone was calling me Preach. I was no longer Greg; I was "the Preach," and I accepted their nickname. (I've been called worse.) Besides, it was a good way to remind me of why I was there while I painted for Jesus.

I began to pray for each of the men I worked with, asking God for opportunities to share Christ. We would all meet in a vacant unit that doubled for a shop in the morning, waiting for the lead foreman to show up and give us our orders. I came to work on Monday after the New Year's weekend after ministering in Oregon. As I walked in the room with several other painters present, one of the guys said, **"What's the good word, Preach?"**

I thought for a minute and said, **"God is good, and His mercy endures forever,"** and I began to talk about His goodness. This began to happen several more times with the question "What's the word for the day?" Each time it led for opportunities to plant seeds of the gospel into their hearts.

I would show up early, park in my van, and pray for each of the men, asking the Holy Spirit to move in our midst. Working with these men gave me a fresh compassion for the lost. I began to see that many times, believers who have come out of the world and have been in church life for a long time, or those raised up in Christian homes, don't know how to react or respond to the lost in a positive way. Many times they become discouraged and overcome by intimidation. They have even, at times, almost alienated themselves from the world, looking for a separation that is not scriptural.

> I wrote unto you in an epistle not to company with fornicators: Yet not altogether with the fornicators of this world, or with the covetous, or extortioners, or with idolaters; for then must ye needs go out of the world.
>
> 1 Corinthians 5:9-10

Paul was talking about those who call themselves Christians and practice such things as explained in verse 11:

> But now I have written unto you not to keep company, if any man that is called a brother be a fornicator, or covetous, or an idolater, or a railer, or a drunkard, or an extortioner; with such an one no not to eat.
>
> 1 Corinthians 5:11
> King James Version

We are not to judge those outside the body; we leave that up to God. Most sinners already know they are lost. We need to bring them the Good News that God isn't mad at them anymore. He loves them and desires them to receive His forgiveness and love demonstrated in the life, death and resurrection of His Son. As someone once said, "Preach the gospel, and not your consecration." Because you and I as Christians may not smoke or drink beer and dance, we preach this to other sinners instead of the gospel. We need to preach the message of the cross and all its benefits, found in a personal relationship with Jesus Christ. God will confirm His word to them through us if we will just speak the truth in love.

One day I was working with two other men in an apartment unit. It was time for break, and so we sat down together on the floor. One of the guys sitting across from me, who had tattoos over most of his body, remarked to the other guy across the room that he didn't feel well. He said, **"I've tried vitamin A, B, and C, and nothing seems to help."** I looked up and said, **"Have you tried vitamin J?"** He replied, **"No, what is vitamin J?"** I replied, **"Vitamin J stands for Jesus, and He said in the Gospel of Mark that believers would lay hands on the sick and they would recover! Do you believe Jesus was telling the truth when**

He spoke these words?" This young man surprised me by saying, **"Jesus would never lie to me."** I replied, **"Would you like me to pray for you?"**

He said yes, so with the other worker watching, I walked over and placed my hand on his head and simply rebuked the fever and commanded the sickness to go. The power of God came on him, and he looked up with a flushed face, exclaiming that all his symptoms were gone! He said it had been a long, long time since he had felt God like that. He began to go around telling the other workers what the Lord had done. The Lord used this healing to help turn this young man around. We began to talk, and I found out he was raised by foster parents who were missionaries and were presently serving the Lord in another nation.

It was awesome to see this young man come alive for the Lord. He began to witness to others about the Lord, sharing with me the joy he felt on the inside. He told me it had been years since he had shared Jesus with anyone. God began to move on the hearts of the workers. Men began to come up to me and ask for prayer for different situations in their lives. One worker, who was on probation, was very worried about his court appearance the next day. I was just about to leave the room when I heard the Holy Spirit tell me to lay hands on him and pray. I asked him if I could pray for him, and when he agreed, I walked over and began to pray Proverbs 21:1: "The King's heart is in the hand of the LORD, like the rivers of water; He turns it wherever He wishes." I asked the Lord to give him favor.

When I finished, I heard another man who was across the room say, **"Preach, would you please pray for me?"** As I came over, he told me, with tears, of his personal struggles and need for prayer. We prayed. Then the most beautiful thing took place. When I had finished praying, he walked over to the other man whom I had prayed for earlier and asked him to forgive him for the things he had said about him. Both these men had been friends, but foolish jesting and gossip had separated them up until now. They both embraced, and forgiveness flowed. The presence of God was so strong in the room, I will never forget that day. I left rejoicing, amazed at what the Holy Spirit had accomplished. It seemed every day God would do something wonderful in our midst.

One morning I was preparing a room to be sprayed when a young man I had witnessed to and prayed for the day before walked over and said, **"You know, I felt good this morning when I came to work. Then I came into this room where you were working to talk to you, and when I went upstairs, I threw up something green on the floor. It looked really weird."** I looked at him, wondering at first what he meant, and then it struck me—he might have just been delivered from an evil spirit because of the anointing. I asked him to show me where he got sick, and when we went up to the room, it was gone, and there was no smell. We both understood then that it was spiritual in nature. God was setting this young man free from the enemy by the power of His anointing. Praise God!

God began to do even more unusual things on the job. Isaiah 28:21 says, "For the LORD will rise up as at Mount Perazim, He will be angry as in the Valley of Gibeon—That He may do His work, His awesome work, and bring to pass His act, His unusual act." Yes, God does unusual things. In the book of Acts, we read where through the hands of the apostles, many signs and wonders were done among the people (Acts 5:12). As believers, we should expect, and be ready for, God to do them, even through us. Mount Perazim is where David inquired of the Lord to wage war against the Philistines. He defeated the Philistines there, as recorded in 2 Samuel 5:19-20. He said the Lord defeated his enemies like the **"breakthrough of waters."** Therefore, he named that place Baal-perazim. As believers filled with the Holy Ghost, we now have rivers of living water that break forth to set the captive free.

Working alone in a room one day, a young man came

142

in holding his stomach and groaning with pain. He said, **"Preach, I don't feel so good; something hurts bad in my stomach."** I asked him if he had eaten anything that morning, and he said not very much. I watched him as he came into the room. I just sort of lifted his name up to the Lord in my heart without speaking out loud. He began to walk around me in a circle, clutching his stomach and moaning. When he got full circle from where he had started, the power of God touched him and he stopped and looked at me, exclaiming with big eyes that the pain was gone. **"Well, give God glory,"** I replied. So he began to thank the Lord!

When he left the room, the Holy Spirit began to talk to me about His desire to heal the sick and touch the lost with His power, even though at times we are not bold to reach out and lay our hands on them. If we would only lift them up in our hearts and pray, we would see God do more.

Word began to get around to the other men working on the project, and opportunity came to witness about Jesus to several. One day I was working in an upper unit with two other guys when I heard a man yelling down the hall, **"Where's Preach? Who's the Preacher?"** The two guys I was with sarcastically told him I was "in my office," pointing into the room I was prepping. I had never talked to him before; he worked for the general contractor doing carpentry work. When he came in, I noticed he was wearing a hard hat with a sticker on it that said, "Jesus saves from hell." He began to tell me of his struggles sharing Christ with a man who was a Jehovah's Witness. "What can I do?" he asked. I began to give him counsel on how to pray and to also stay clear of arguments and just to share Who Jesus was to him and what He had done personally in his own life. I told him I would be praying and we would talk later. As soon as he left, another man who needed prayer came seeking me out. When he left, the two other painters in the unit came over to me and said they were going to build me a confessional and start taking offerings. We all had a pretty good laugh.

I must admit, I began to get a little concerned because I was there to do a job, and I didn't want to bring any reproach to the Lord by stopping and spending time to pray when I should be working. I decided the best thing to do was to try to encourage them to meet me at lunch or break for counseling or prayer.

One such time was when a young man who had just started working with me came over to me and said, "Why do they call you preach?" I smiled and told him I was inclined to do that from time to time. We got to be friends. He was a really big guy from a small town in Nebraska. The guys on the crew nicknamed him "Corn Fed," but not to his face. One day he came up to me and remarked about a feeling of peace he felt whenever he was around me. I told him about the peace that comes from knowing the Lord Jesus. After a couple of days of sharing the Word when there was opportunity and answering some of the questions he had about God and the Bible, he opened up to reveal his spiritual hunger. He told me how he had been to church before and was reading his Bible to his daughter at night before she went to bed, but something was still missing. I told him I would talk to him more at break time since we both needed to get back to work. When break came, I began to share the gospel with him. As break was over, I suggested we get together the next day during lunch and continue our discussion. He agreed, and I began to pray for him the rest of the day and at home, looking forward to our next meeting.

I sensed in my spirit this man was ready to accept the Lord, and so I prayed, looking forward to our meeting. The next day at lunch, we were supposed to meet, but the devil got in and discouraged him, and he went somewhere else to eat with another worker. I knew I needed to get more prayer going, so I encouraged Bill, a believer full of the Holy Spirit and the Word, to pray. Bill was not always assigned to work on the same job site with me, but it was good encouragement and fellowship whenever he was around. The following day, the young man I was supposed to meet with came up and apologized for not making the meeting. He was very discouraged, but I smiled and told him it was okay and said, "Let's try meeting today." At noon, during lunch, he showed up, and we spent about twenty minutes talking and looking at the Bible verses on salvation. I asked him if he was ready to give his life to Jesus, and he said, "Yes."

I led him in a prayer to receive Christ, and after we prayed, I laid hands on him and the Holy Spirit came upon him and he began to experience some of the joy of the Lord. He remarked about feeling warm all over and kind of lightheaded. Then He asked me if he could go home and pray the same prayer with his wife. He wanted to know if He could use the same Scriptures to help her find God. I was so blessed to hear this new convert ready to step out and bring Christ to his wife and family. Salvation had come to his home! We began to meet at lunchtime and study the Word together. We had times of prayer in my van when the fire of God would show up. He would remark about the heat and fire he felt on his body. He had never experienced this kind of manifestation before. God was good to confirm His Word with signs and wonders.

The Lord did many wonderful things during my time there, planting seeds of the gospel, healing the sick, and setting souls free. It was a wonderful time. Eventually, after ten months, God began to talk to me about leaving and starting my own painting company. I told the Lord I wanted an opportunity to speak to the entire crew before I left. The answer to that prayer request came in two weeks. But never in the way I would have wanted or expected.

It was Monday, and I had given my two weeks' notice and was working my final week. It was around ten o'clock when the job foreman, Bob, came into the room where I was working. He had a very sad countenance, and there were tears in his eyes. He told me Jim's son (Jim was another painter on the crew) had been involved in an accidental shooting on

Saturday and had died Sunday evening. He said the father was home and wanted me to come to the house and speak to the family. We left the job site immediately, and I followed him in my car. As I drove to the home, I prayed, "What do I say to a man who has just lost his son? Lord, please help, I don't know what to say!" I began praying in the spirit and asking God to give me wisdom and compassion for this man and his family. "Lord, help me to speak Your words of grace and healing to this family," I prayed.

When we arrived, Bob introduced me to the family. The father, who worked with us, had been out walking. He came in as I was in the living room. I found myself walking over and embracing him. We both wept. In times like these, words aren't always the most important thing; just being there and showing you care can bring a lot of support and strength. We walked out back and sat on the patio, and he shared what had happened.

His son had been with his buddies at his wife's place. (They were presently separated.) Another young man wanted to show the young man the gun he had in his car. He pulled it out from under the seat of the car, and, as he did, it accidentally fired. The gun was a large-caliber revolver, and it shot him in the chest. His older brother heard the shot and came running over, seeing him lying on the ground with a bullet in the chest. He held him in his arms and tried to stop the bleeding. Because of the gun shot, when the police arrived, they set up a barrier down the street, so the aid car did not get to the victim until after the police had made their way up to the site and safely cleared the area of any further danger. By that time, the young man had lost a lot of blood. He never recovered and eventually died later in the hospital.

We sat on his back porch, and I listened as he told me of his love for his son. There were lots of unanswered questions in his heart. I told him that what had happened was not God's best for him. As a matter of fact, to be honest, I simply said the whole thing stunk. I said if anyone was to blame, it was the devil, and we needed to look to Jesus and receive His grace to go on. The devil came to steal, kill, and destroy, but Jesus came so we might have life and have it more abundantly. Then I told him that his son was in a better place. At first I was taken aback by why I would make such a claim not personally knowing of his son's spiritual life. I do not normally make such statements.

How could I know if he was in heaven? Was God showing me something? Later God would confirm this. I told Jim about King David, who, when faced with the death of his son from Bathsheba, said, "He cannot come to me, but I may go to him." We have a hope in Christ that we will be reunited with our loved ones once again. We spent some time talking, and then we prayed. Jim left with his wife to make the necessary funeral arrangements, and I stayed with Bob and the rest of his family. The Holy Spirit was really at work on Bob's heart. The present circumstances opened the door to talk about life and death and what the Bible had to say.

At one point, he asked me how a person gets born again, and I shared the plan of salvation with him. I asked him if he was ready to receive Christ. Bob said he wasn't ready because he wanted to come to God on his own terms, and he knew God wanted him to come on His terms. I told him I appreciated his insight and honesty. You should never pressure someone to give his or her life to Christ; if you do, you will only have a decision, not a conversion. Yet I knew in my heart Bob was very close to the kingdom. I stayed at Jim's home for some time talking to Bob and then eventually left and drove home.

The atmosphere at work the next day was very somber. The death of Jim's son had a profound effect on the crew. I sensed throughout the morning that the Lord was going to open a door for me to minister at the funeral. Later on that day, the foreman informed me Jim wanted me to call him after work to discuss funeral services. The company I worked for gave all the employees the option to work or attend the funeral service on Wednesday. Tuesday evening, I called Jim, and he asked me if I would bring a message at the chapel and graveside services. After talking with Jim and praying for him, I hung up the phone and began to seek the Lord as to what He would have me say.

I knew my first priority was to bring words of healing and peace to the family. I didn't want to view this as just an opportunity to have a captive audience to preach to. Sometimes we can be overzealous and insensitive in our desire to see friends and family members come to Christ and do something like giving an "evangelistic" sermon at mealtime when we're just supposed to be saying grace over the food. Yet I also wanted to be obedient to whatever the Holy Spirit would have me say and do. In prayer that evening, I again had, as earlier, a real sense in my spirit that this young teenager was not lost, but with the Lord in heaven. As I prayed, the Holy Spirit gave me John 12:24: "Most assuredly, I say to you, unless a grain of wheat falls into the ground and dies, it remains alone; but if it dies, it produces much grain."

The Lord wanted me to see the death of Jim's son as a grain of wheat. His death would bring forth fruit for the kingdom of God. God was going to take what the devil meant for evil and bring glory to His name. Again I had the sense that Jim's son was in heaven with Christ. I knew he was beyond my judgment, but how and when did he receive Jesus as Savior and Lord? I began to pray for the service, asking God to use me in any way He wanted.

The day of the funeral, I left my home an hour before the service to meet with the funeral director and family of the young man who was killed. I was not prepared for what I saw when I drove up. The funeral home was crowded with lots of people, young and old. When I walked in, I met many of the guys I had been working with. We all remarked how different we looked in dress suits instead of our painter whites. This helped lighten the atmosphere. The entrance to the funeral home was packed with high school kids wearing white T-shirts that had a picture of the young man on the front with "R.I.P. Justin" on the back, showing his birth and death dates. Rap music was playing throughout the foyer. There were lots of gang-type kids walking around looking lost, some quietly crying, and others just standing alone, staring. I prayed, asking the Holy Spirit to come and comfort these young people who were here to pay respect to their friend. After meeting with the funeral director, I found out, per the family's request, there was going to be a Catholic priest at 12:00 to lead the rosary, and then I would speak at 1 P.M. When I met with the father of the young man who had been killed, Bob, the foreman, was also present. Jim began to tell Bob, in my presence, the reason God had sent "Preach" to work with us was because God knew we would need him for this hour. I was humbled and again made aware that you and I have been ordained of God for such a time as this. We need to understand that wherever God has placed us, we are there to be a light for those who don't know Jesus.

After we talked, I went into the room where the minister usually waits until they call him to the podium. Shortly after that, the Catholic priest came in and introduced himself. He left and went to start the service. As I began to pray, the door burst open, and Jim came into the room, followed by a man carrying a woman who was pregnant and in pain.

She had fainted in the chapel. I cleared the chairs, and the man laid her on the floor. She began to exclaim she was discharging. Fearing a miscarriage and wanting to give his wife privacy, the man who did not know me looked at me and asked me to leave. Jim said, "No, this is Preach, he needs to pray." The young woman was Jim's relative. I laid my hands on her and commanded the pain to go and spoke peace to her womb and a prayer of protection over the baby. The pain subsided, and she lay resting on the floor. The funeral director had called the paramedics, and they arrived shortly to examine the women. I left the room and went looking for a place to be alone and pray. The only place available was the restroom. At least I could escape the chants of rosary coming through the speaker system. I began to pray and intercede, binding the religious spirit that was charging the atmosphere with such unbelief. I needed the Holy Spirit to come and bring the Father's love and the light of the gospel into this place. Finally, the priest was done, and he left the chapel. I was saddened that he said nothing to bring healing or peace to all those people in the chapel. No hope, no gospel, no words of faith. I do not mean to be critical of this Catholic priest. I realize there are many who know the Lord and are filled with the Holy Spirit. This man missed the opportunity. God help us to speak words of grace and truth when they need to be spoken.

The funeral director told me there would be a short recess and I would be next. I looked around, and the place had filled up with more people. The chapel was packed, with nowhere else to sit, and the foyer was filled with young people hanging out by the entrance doors and on the sidewalk in front of the building. What could I do so those who were standing outside the chapel could hear the message? I decided to ask the director if we could open up both double doors leading into the foyer so those in that room could see and hear and if we could allow the young people to come and sit on the floor around the front of the chapel. Praise the Lord! He agreed and began to invite them in.

When it came time for me to speak, I walked in and stood behind the podium, looking at all those faces. The young people were gathered around the floor up to where I stood. As I looked out to the foyer, I could see the faces of more young people pressing to get a view. I was so grateful for the grace and power of the Holy Spirit to help me. The anointing came as I opened my mouth and began to share. He gave me just the right words to say. I addressed the family members with their grief and the question, How do we, when faced with tragedy, continue to go on affirming life and faith in God?, telling them of the hope we have in Christ and the victory won for us at the cross. The Holy Spirit brought words of grace and truth. Eventually, I opened up the microphone to give opportunity for any of the family members or friends to share what was on their heart. Several came up to plea for an end to the violence and to put their guns away. One young man began to tell his young friends to listen to what I was telling them about God and His love.

When I came back to the podium, I began to share the Good News, speaking the Word and sharing in terms that were simple. I trusted the Holy Spirit to move on each heart. When I gave the altar call, inviting them to give their lives to Jesus, hands began to go up all around the chapel and the foyer. I don't know how many hands were raised, but I did ask everyone to repeat the words of repentance and confession in Christ as we joined together to pray. I watched in joy as my job foreman, Bob, raised his hands among them that day. Glory!

After the altar call, I mentioned there would be a short graveside service and then closed the service. I walked over to the parents of the young man and was greeted by the father, who was rejoicing over the many young people who had responded to the altar call. I told him of the Scripture the Lord had given me in John's Gospel about their son being like a seed planted and that his death was not in vain, but God had truly used his death to bring forth fruit. That is when I was told how this young man had gone with his mother to a Benny Hinn crusade at the Tacoma Dome just several months earlier and had gone forward to receive Jesus Christ into his heart. Glory to God! He was in heaven! He may not have been discipled like he should have been in those first couple of months, and, yes, he was in the wrong place at the wrong time and lost his life, but God, in His mercy, had saved his soul before he slipped into eternity. God is good!

We as believers need to remember that God is inside of us! Emmanuel dwells in us. Many Christians can quote Isaiah 52:7, and we even sing it in our church services: "How lovely on the mountains are the feet of him who brings good news, who announces peace and brings good news of happiness, who announces salvation, and says to Zion, 'Your God reigns!' "

But not many consider or know verse 7, which is the reason why the feet of those who bring good news are lovely. Look at what it says: "Therefore My people shall know My name; therefore in that day I am the one who is speaking, 'Here I am.' "

He said in that day, God is the One Who is speaking, "Here I am." Here comes God in the person of the Holy Spirit on the inside of you and me, announcing the gospel! No wonder our feet are described as being lovely! Not just because of us, but because of Christ in us! The hope of glory! Wherever God sends you and I, God goes with us. Remember what Jesus said when He sent out His disciples:

> For it is not you who speak, but it is the Spirit
> of your Father who speaks in you.
>   Matthew 10:20

Go ahead! Step out in faith, knowing God will give you the words to say to that neighbor, or that one at the workplace, or the stranger you meet along the way.

Begin your adventure of being a witness for Christ.

> And Jesus came up and spoke to them,
> saying, "All authority has been given to Me
> in heaven and on earth. Go therefore and
> make disciples of all the nations, baptizing
> them in the name of the Father and the Son
> and the Holy Spirit, teaching them to observe
> all that I commanded you; and lo, I am with

you always, even to the end of the age."
Matthew 28:18-20

You are never alone when you share you faith. I shared earlier what Luke wrote in Acts 5:32, that we are His witnesses and so also is the Holy Spirit Whom God has given to those who obey Him. When we obey the promptings of the Spirit of God, we will see the Lord manifested in many wonderful ways. One such way happened while I was in downtown Seattle, helping a young man get his life on track by taking him to see his probation officer. I had some time to kill before I needed to pick him up, and so I walked over to Pike Place Market. It is a great place to browse and shop and take in some lunch. While walking around, I began to pray, asking the Father to let me be a vessel for His love to flow through. As I was walking through the market area, I came to a certain storefront and just stepped back from the sidewalk away from the street in front of the open market behind me. I quietly prayed in the spirit as I watched the people shopping and walking by just a few steps in front of me. Shortly thereafter, an elderly lady came down the sidewalk, shuffling toward me, using a walker to help her move. I was just praying and looking to the Lord when she got right in front of me and said out loud, looking straight ahead and not at me, **"I wish these legs would work."** Many times Jesus knew their thoughts, but here it was as if the Lord was having her speak out loud the thoughts she had in her heart for me to hear. I responded by saying, **"What is wrong with your legs?"** She stopped and looked at me kind of puzzled, and I said again, **"Your legs, you said they don't work."** She replied, **"Yes,"** kind of embarrassed, and so I said, **"I am a Christian, and I believe Jesus Christ wants to heal your legs. Can I pray for you?"** She said, **"Yes,"** so I simply stepped next to her and put my hand on her shoulder and said, **"In the name of Jesus, I rebuke the spirit of infirmity and command your legs to be healed."**

I did not shout or make a big scene, just a prayer spoken out loud in faith. Then I said, **"Start moving your legs up and down."** She immediately started marching in place, and then a big smile came on her face!

I asked her, **"What did Jesus do?"** And she replied her legs felt a lot better and were more limber and asked if I also would pray about her diabetic condition. So we prayed into that, and after talking some more and fellowshipping, she walked off, rejoicing in the goodness of the Lord and her newfound freedom.

The Bible says in Acts 10:38, **"How God anointed Jesus of Nazareth with the Holy Spirit and with power who went about doing good and healing all who were oppressed by the devil, for God was with Him."** I always have believed I could claim that verse for me as I go about in my Father's name doing good. I like to say, "How God anointed Greg Daley, who went about doing good…for God was with Him." I know that was Jesus! That is true, but Jesus is our example, and we are called to walk with Him. Did He not say in John 14:12-13, **"The works that I do shall you do also and greater works shall you do because I go unto the Father. And whatsoever you shall ask in my name, that will I do, that the Father may be glorified in the Son"**?

In fact, a man name Bullinger, who wrote most of the notes in the Companion Bible, said that there were fifty-two times in the New Testament where the term "Holy Ghost" should literally be translated, not the person of the Holy Ghost, but the manifestation of the Holy Ghost, and Acts 10:38 is one of those verses. Jesus received the Spirit in fullness, with nothing held back, and He alone has universal authority. However, since this endowment of the Holy Spirit is given to Him Whom God has sent (John 3:34), there is a similar unlimited resource of Holy Spirit fullness available to all obedient disciples of Jesus Christ.

The Gospel of John in chapter four says: "He left Judea and departed again to Galilee. But He needed to go through

Samaria." Jesus' need to go through Samaria was not merely for a good travel route, but a divine compulsion. His Father in heaven saw this woman coming to the well and knew if He got His Son to this divine appointment, not only would she believe in the Son, but revival would come to an entire town. Jesus walked in perfect divine activity. He was about His Father's business. You and I are called to this kind of activity as we go about our daily lives of being open to the Spirit's leading. Evangelism is a lifestyle.

> Now thanks be to God who always leads us in triumph in Christ. And through us manifests the fragrance of His knowledge in every place.
>
> 2 Corinthians 2:14

I like the way *The Message* puts it:

> Thank God! In the Messiah, in Christ, God leads us from place to place in one perpetual victory parade. Through us, he brings knowledge of Christ. Everywhere we go, people breathe in the exquisite fragrance.
>
> 2 Corinthians 2:14

What a joy, yet what a responsibility we have to bring the Good News to those who do not know Jesus. Proverbs 24:11-12 is a somber reminder of this responsibility: "Deliver those who are drawn toward death, and hold back those stumbling to the slaughter. If you say, 'Surely we did not know this,' does not He who weighs the hearts consider it? He who keeps your soul, does He not know it? And will He not render to each man according to his deeds?"

Have you ever looked at the obituaries in the newspaper or been to a funeral of a friend or relative? The big question is not, "Why did they die?" but "Where are they?" Everyone dies someday and will live forever somewhere—either with Christ in His kingdom or in hell, separated forever from the love of God. Proverbs 11:30 says, "The fruit of the righteous is a tree of life, and he who wins souls is wise." It takes wisdom to win one soul, much less many. The Hebrew word translated "win" is *laqach* (law-kak). The root word means to "take" in the widest variety of applications. To accept, bring, buy, carry away, drawn, fetch, get, even to seize!

The Holy Spirit will use us in many ways to win the lost as we yield our lives to Him. We so need to preach the Word, for "It was God's good pleasure through the foolishness of the preaching to save them that believe" (1 Corinthians 1:21). We also need to remember to speak the truth in love and to walk in wisdom toward those who are without Christ. James 3:17 says, "the wisdom that comes from above is first pure, then peaceable, gentle, willing to yield, full of mercy and good fruits, without partiality and without hypocrisy." His agape flowing out of our hearts and His wisdom will help us to bridge the gap of unbelief that separates them from the Father's love. Before John G. Lake died, he had a vision of the final move of the Holy Spirit. Out of that vision, he prophesied these words: **"I can see...that there is coming from heaven a new manifestation of the Holy Spirit in power and that new manifestation will be in sweetness, in love, in tenderness, beyond anything your heart or mine ever saw. The very lightning of God will flash through men's souls."**

Love is the greatest need of mankind—to know the Father's love and to receive Him into our hearts, for God is love. John G. Lake believed and preached that "as He is so are we in this world" (1 John 4:17). Lake also used Isaiah 61:1-3 as his platform for ministry. As I close this book, I would like to paraphrase for you what Jesus said when he went into the synagogue on the Sabbath day and stood up to read. I would ask you to make it your prayerful declaration as you go into all the world with the spirit of reconciliation and share what you have both seen and heard—that Jesus is the Christ, the Messiah, and the soon-coming King.

I know that heaven has been silent for hundreds of years. I know that since Malachi until now you have not seen a move of God, but here is Isaiah 61:1, and I'm quoting it to you: "The Spirit of the Lord is upon Me, because He has anointed Me to do these things. I am going to heal the brokenhearted, preach recovering of sight to the blind. I am going to bring a miracle move, because I am going to preach the acceptable year of the Lord – the Jubilee Year – the year where God is active, the year and the hour where man no longer needs to wait for a future date in God.

Printed in the United States
42743LVS00003B/1-177

9 781597 816939